THE VALKYRIES:
The Women Around Jung

Maggy Anthony trained in analytical
psychology at the C.G. Jung Institute in
Zurich, and now lives in America where she
lectures in Jungian psychology, Egyptian
mythology, dreams, matriarchal religions and
native American spirituality.

THE VALKYRIES:
THE WOMEN AROUND JUNG

MAGGY ANTHONY

Element Books

First published in Great Britain in 1990 by
Element Books Limited
Longmead, Shaftesbury, Dorset

Cover photograph: Museo Nazionale delle Terme, Rome
Cover design by Max Fairbrother
Designed by Nancy Lawrence

Typeset in Baskerville by Input Typesetting Ltd,
London SW19 8DR
Printed and bound in Great Britain by
Billings Ltd, Hylton Road, Worcester

British Library Cataloguing in Publication Data
Anthony, Maggy
The Valkyries : the women around Jung.
1. Psychoanalysis. Jung, C. G. (Carl Gustav) 1875–1961.
Interpersonal relationships with women
I. Title
150.195

ISBN 1–85230–187–2

This book is dedicated to the memory
of
Bettilou Cosgrove O'Leary
1929–72

Contents

Acknowledgements

There are so many people who aided me in the writing
of this book that my fear is that I will leave one of them
out.

First of all my children, now wonderful, intelligent adult
friends, Anna Anthony Krave and Joshua Anthony, who
travelled uncomplainingly (most of the time) to foreign
lands and who shared with me the wonders and despairs
of my search for an authentic life. Their love has made
it all worthwhile. Stephen Kathriner, who by his long-
term friendship and presence at all my interviews lent his
gentle perspective from the introverted feeling place to
neatly balance my extroverted intuition. Thanks to my
brother, Lou O'Leary, who first told me in 1963 of a
wonderful book, *Memories, Dreams, Reflections*, which started
me on my Jungian journey, to his wife, Judith Graves
O'Leary, and to both of them for their unfailing financial
and moral support from the beginning of this venture.
My friends have given me immeasurable support and
understanding: I am grateful to Philip Culjak for his
listening skills and for his contribution in terms of astro-
logical knowledge and intelligent criticism; Sandra Lehti
Culjak for taking me out to play when I was immersed
in the despair and delight of writing and for giving me
courage to begin again and again when I faltered; Boone
Lodge and Bill Sullivan for their financial support and
unreserved friendship through thick and thin, and it was
pretty thin at times; Vanita and Danny Linthicum and
their family for their unconditional love; Bob McClay for
his creative response to all my various undertakings and
his great sense of humour that gave me perspective
through the dark times; to my analyst, Dr Charles Poncé,

for his intuitive genius and his willingness to take risks, and for his nurturing of my creative side when I would have let it wither; and to Maggie Bome who came up with £100 and a half pint of bitter at a critical moment in the Cotswolds.

I would also like to thank all the inquisitive, intelligent people throughout the western United States who have come to my lectures and classes over the past twenty years, stimulating my creativity further.

Lastly, my thanks to Dr R. James Yandell, former President of the C.G. Jung Institute of San Francisco, for his belief in me when I could not believe in myself. Although he is in no way responsible for the opinions and conclusions drawn in this book, he was instrumental in its beginnings.

Introduction

The beginnings of this book go back over the years to a grey day in the spring of 1977. I was sitting in a café in Eugene, Oregon, drinking coffee to warm myself. I had just come from the hospital where my mother lay in the long process of dying. I was in a philosophical mood, no doubt as a result of the questions that arise when one is faced with the imminent death of a parent. I was thinking of my mother's last few years and regretting how bitter and angry she had become, after having been the rather cheerful, fun-loving figure of my childhood.

Images of ageing women came into my mind: women whom I had met during a study year in Zurich at the C.G. Jung Institute, women whose books on analytical psychology I had read; women whose lectures I had attended at the Analytical Psychology Club meetings. What was the secret of their longevity? How had they managed to stay vital and interested, often into their eighties and nineties?

As I pondered these questions I wondered if there was any guidance there for me on how I might live my life, and avoid the frustration that could lead to the life-threatening bitterness and anger of my mother's last years. Unavoidably, I was led to the conclusion that the secret of their lives must, in some way, lie in their commitment to the psychology of Jung and possibly to Jung himself.

All great men have legends that have grown up around them after they die, obscuring the human being that was there in life. This is no less true of C.G. Jung, but the stories that are prized most are those that point up his earthiness, his peasant-like robustness and his simplicity. These seem to be told to balance the certainty among the women who survived him that while Jung lived, a genius walked among them and befriended them. The tone is often that of a mother who is almost bewildered by her son's greatness, nevertheless very certain of it.

Women came from all over the world to see him, starting from before the First World War. They came from Austria, Germany, Israel, but most often, England and America. Their journey took on a mythical quality, almost like a religious pilgrimage. They came to be healed, and often something happened that made them stay and become healers in their turn. Many of them stayed to remain close to Jung, the 'lifeline', and to help in any way they could. Others returned home but came back periodically for times of renewal with him. Every one of them felt that he had saved her life. These were the women who became what I have called (after others) the Valkyries. They were the group of women who gathered around Jung through the years, or who were, perhaps unconsciously, gathered by him, and who remained spiritually and psychically close all their lives. After his death, many of them remained close through their dreams and visions.

They were women who came to a strong man to find their own strength in an era when it was not 'nice' for a woman to be strong; women were merely useful. Through their experiences of Jung as a person and as an analyst, they came to terms with their strength, finding a channel for it and a closed society that accepted them. They made lives for themselves, but seemed always to need to be linked to the man who helped them give birth to themselves.

At the time I first went to the Institute for Analytical Psychology, many of these women were still active within it, teaching, giving analysis, and helping in a practical sense. My observance of these women and the tremendous personal vitality that radiated from them made me more curious about the man who had drawn them to himself and to his psychology. At that time, Marie-Louise von Franz, the late Jolande Jacobi, Liliane Frey-Rohn, the late Barbara Hannah and many others less publicly known were still active. As time wore on, I began to be as interested in them as in Dr Jung himself. I was to learn in writing this book that they were inseparable subjects: that I couldn't do a book about them that wouldn't touch constantly upon his life, as his life had touched theirs at every step after they met.

I was also to learn, to my surprise, of the furore caused by my attempting to write this book at all. I was threatened, told that I would never be able to do anything in the field of psychology in California if the book was published and that the Jungians would make it difficult for me to do anything at all. All this by respected Jungian psychologists whom I had allowed to read my first draft. Puzzled, I re-read the book myself and was still at a loss to see what had incurred their wrath. Then I realised what was the main cause: that I dared to write *anything at all* concerning Jung. 'How dare you try to analyse Jung? What right have *you* to do such a thing?' This was how one of my enraged readers put it. At the time I was at a loss to reply, taken aback by the passion behind the questions. But of course I dared.

This book was born in the welter of questions I had in my mind: Why had Jung and his psychology attracted so many women? What had his psychology to do with their longevity? What myths, which his psychology had categorised, had made their presence felt in the relationship?

At first I thought these questions would be easy enough to answer if I interviewed those women still alive; I would find out as much from their evasiveness as from their answers. I had not reckoned with their almost universal introversion. In Jungian terms, most of the women (apart from Jolande Jacobi) were deeply introverted (that is, they were more interested in their own inner processes than in the outer world), and the most generalised questions were regarded as gross invasions of privacy. 'I will talk to you about Jung, but I will not discuss anything personal', was the general reply. Secondly, they were very wary, with some justification, of the American process of popularisation which tends to trivialise.

In any case, material from the women themselves was

slow in coming. Much of it had to be rooted out from the writings in the various journals of Jungian thought and from the women's obituaries. This led to the inevitable exclusion of many of the women for lack of information, notably Aniela Jaffé, Liliane Frey-Rohn, and many others. Less reticent to speak were many of the Jungian men who noted, sometimes humorously, sometimes resentfully, the interplay between Jung and the women. Jung's family was determined that personal information about their father and grandfather should not become public.

I have therefore looked for clarification in the small anecdotes that are part of a friendly atmosphere, to the psychology of Jung himself, and I have also read between the lines of written accounts of certain festivities and meetings. Perhaps this method will ultimately bring us closer to the truth since memories themselves can be the greatest deceivers.

It is because of my own admiration and fascination with Jung's psychology and his almost mystical vision, that I 'dare' to write this book at all, even though I am not an analyst. Ultimately the strength of this book may rest in the fact that it is written not by a Jungian 'expert', but merely by an interested bystander whose own life has been profoundly touched and enriched by the psychology of C.G. Jung.

CHAPTER ONE

A Forum is Created

In the autumn of 1948, after over thirty years of working in the protected atmosphere of a small, closely-knit group, shielded from an often confused and hostile public, Jung and his circle opened their doors to the world. It was an exciting day, but the excitement was expressed in that repressed way that is very Swiss. The old building on the Gemeindestrasse with the staid Victorian exterior seemed to belie the momentousness of the occasion. Symbolically, the doors opened, not on to the street, but into a small, sheltered courtyard that had to be entered from the pavement. It was located near the street of the Mother Goddess and the street of the Goddess of Wisdom: Junostrasse and Minervastrasse.

As each student pressed the outside bell, Fräulein Amman would come to the massive wooden door, open it cautiously and enquire as to who was there and what was the nature of their business. It must have seemed rather more like requesting an audience with the Pope than attending a place of higher education. The confused accents of the young American students, the homely Schweizer-Deutsch of the Zurich students, and the more formal High German of the doctors and professors swept over the impassive countenance of this human watchdog as she conducted them to a small classroom inside. Fräulein Amman would then retire to the tiny kitchen to begin preparations for the coffee to be served midway through the class.

Every once in a while, the secretary, Fräulein Jaffé, would peek nervously into the subdued classroom to see if all were gathered yet.

At last the door opened and Frau Jolande Jacobi, a

1

petite, well-dressed woman, walked in and went to the podium. She glanced nervously at the twelve students who had gathered and seated themselves, somewhat defensively, at the back of the classroom. She smiled a bit tremulously at them and said, 'Please. Come to the front of the room. I'm an extrovert and I like to have people around me.' In spite of the obvious strength that emanated from her, it was apparent she needed the support of the students. Reluctantly they gathered their books and papers and slowly made their ways to the front of the classroom. The first day of the C.G. Jung Institute for Analytical Psychology had begun.

In the weeks that followed, nervousness was the dominant feature of the teaching staff, which was made up of those women who were part of the inner circle around Jung from the earliest days of his career. This nervousness was largely due to the fact that for the first time they were presenting material to people *outside* their charmed circle. The composition of the teaching staff changed over the years as new teachers came in and others returned periodically to their home countries to spread the Jungian word there. But in general they were known to the student by several irreverent nicknames: the Vestal Virgins, the Maenads, the Jungfrauen, and the Valkyries.

According to one of the many American students of the early days of the Institute, nervousness seemed rather out of character in these otherwise intellectually formidable women. However, in retrospect, it can be appreciated that the business of becoming public, after Jung and his thought had been almost a family affair for decades previously, would almost certainly make for tension. Jung himself was an introvert, as were almost all those in his circle. Public contact was not something that was necessarily desired outside of their analytical work. They had become used to the support that teaching and presenting papers to a small group of like minds provided. The glare of the public eye would not be enjoyed.

Two years before, in 1946, Dr Jacobi, the unofficial Jungian extravert, had pressed Dr Jung to start an institute. Jung had been horrified at the idea. Dr Jacobi knew that such an institute would eventually come into being anyway, after Jung's death. She argued to him that should they wait too long, he would not be able to exert his influence in constructing it along lines which he felt appropriate.

So Jung capitulated. He felt that if he could be around at its inception, he might spare it from the more obvious mistakes. He himself chose the first Curatorium or Board of Directors. On it he put two men, C.A. Meier and Ludwig Binswanger, both distinguished analysts. He chose two of the more outgoing women for the other members: Dr Jacobi and Liliane Frey-Rohn. There was a great deal of controversy over his choice of Dr Jacobi. As we shall see later, she was not popular among the members of the Zurich Psychological Club. Jung had his way, naturally, claiming she was the most adept of them all in dealing with the public. Dr Joseph Henderson has referred to her as the Sol Hurok[1] of Jungian affairs, and maintains that she was a most exasperating woman who grated on the nerves of the more introverted Jungians.

Perhaps there was a small amount of jealousy over her natural ability to charm people. Whether she was difficult or not, much of the Institute was created from her prodigious energies.

It soon became evident that the Institute was a showcase for the variety of talents and personalities of the women around Jung. And, more than any of his male contemporaries, it was women who seemed particularly drawn to his work and personality. Some reasons for this were more apparent than others. One reason was that, at the beginning of the century women were still very much second-class citizens. As Dr Liliane Frey-Rohn has put it, 'Women were still thought to be without souls.'[2] Few creative men, during the first half of this century, took women seriously at all, still less would they willingly take them on as collaborators or assistants, though they might just find them useful as 'muses'.

Jung, from the beginning, took women seriously, mainly because of his own psychological make-up, as we shall see. He wrote an article in the early 1920s entitled, 'Women in

3

Europe', which was to attract many of his female followers in spite of such sexist remarks as 'No one can get around the fact that by taking up a masculine profession, studying and working like a man, woman is doing something not wholly in accord with, if not directly injurious to her feminine nature', or 'It is a woman's outstanding characteristic that she can do anything for the love of a man. But these women who achieve something important for the love of doing a thing are exceptional because this really does not agree with their nature. Love for a thing is a man's prerogative.'[3] These remarks must be taken in the context of the times and may have seemed mild enough to the women.

He was also a very dynamic and physically attractive man, and this cannot be underestimated as part of his power. He was bursting with physical and mental vitality which made him appear to be a natural healer of souls. The mechanism in his personal psychology which made him particularly vulnerable and open to women must also be taken into consideration.

From the very beginnings of his private practice, Jung had a disproportionately large number of women patients. Although attractiveness played its part, another reason may have been his difficulties in relating closely to men. He admits this in a letter to Freud.[4] Many of the men whom I interviewed felt that he was an overwhelming figure, whose sheer force of personality and stature made them feel unimportant. Most of the men got away as soon as possible so their own lights could shine.

The women came as patients and many remained as analysts, colleagues or helpers of one sort or another, particularly the unmarried ones. His vitality, good looks and the impression of being larger than life did not threaten them, but merely added to their attachment to him. He was also very much in touch, through his important relationship with his mother, with what is traditionally described in Jungian thought as the feminine side of his nature, or anima. Observers have said that he was very aware of his effect upon women and felt it entailed a responsibility from which he never tried to escape. It might be said that he never did anything to discourage it either. 'He never let you down.'[5] He did still hold to the view prevalent at the time that women related to life solely through men. But he also felt that it was important that women have their own work, though one has the impression that this was to prevent the full force of the mother's and wife's energies focusing on husband and children to the detriment of the latter. The fear of women was in Jung too, it seems.

A young man, coming to Jung shortly before the Second World War, was indignant about the women who seemed to form a human cordon around him. He said something to the effect that he didn't see how Jung could stand 'those old girls' fluttering around him. Jung became very angry and told him that every one of the women was doing important and creative work and that not only were they a help to him, but they were furthering the knowledge and understanding of psychology. He went on to say that they had come to him when they had not been able to function very well, but now they could. He admitted that they seemed to need a lifeline to him and that as long as he saw them once every three months, six months or a year, they could function well. He added that he loved and respected these women even though *it was a burden being the spiritual father who energised them*, and kept them in equilibrium so they could keep on doing their good work. 'Wait until you are my age and if you don't have a few of these "old girls" hanging around, I'll be surprised. . . . And by that time you will have changed your attitude toward them.'[6]

This reveals much about Jung and his attitude to the women around him. From the journal of another man[7] we hear that: 'Unkind gossip has accused these disciples and auditors of snobbery. But when someone raised the objection that a majority of his disciples were women, Jung is said to have replied, "What's to be done? Psychology after all is the science of the soul, and it is not my fault if the soul is a woman." A jest; but for anyone who has followed his teaching, a jest which is itself charged with experience.'

5

All this suggests that Jung felt the women needed his presence, even if only in the form of an occasional visit, for their continued well-being. This is a very shamanistic view in its acceptance that the very physical presence of the healer is capable of healing. It suggests, too, that the transference (whereby the analysand works out unresolved conflicts on the analyst) was never completely abandoned, nor did Jung expect it to be. One begins to wonder to what degree it was mutual: did Jung need these women's support as much as they needed his?

Jung, following in the classical humanist tradition, needed his 'femme inspiratrice', or creative muse. He lived in the same cultural tradition as did his 'ancestor' Goethe, and still called upon women as sources of inspiration.

Jung's psychology stems from an awareness of the mythic material operating in the psyche. There are indications that one of the myths operating in his own personality was that of Pygmalion, indications of which keep cropping up in the women's descriptions of him (see Chapter Fifteen). Mention is consistently made of the fact that he was adept at helping women patients find themselves and their 'greater personalities'. When they had dreamt of him as a wizard or wise old man, he would say, 'Good. Excellent! Now that you have dreamed it, it shows you have the potential within yourself.' As one woman has put it, 'With Jung you didn't have to be someone famous or special or unusual. He treated you as if you *were* special.' At a time when ambitious women were frowned upon and felt to be somehow unnatural, Jung realised that they needed intellectual outlets.

To find the true beginnings of the circle of women which eventually formed around him, we must go to the earliest days of Jung's fascination with Woman and the role she played in Man's psyche. We must also go to Jung's struggle, not always successful, with the psyches of women. Seen psychologically, this fascination undoubtedly began with his mother, Emilie Preiswerk Jung.

Notes

1. Dr Joseph Henderson, author's interview, November 1977.
2. Dr Liliane Frey-Rohn, author's interview, June 1978.
3. *The Collected Works of C.G. Jung*, Vol. 10.
4. W. McGuire (ed.) *The Freud/Jung Letters*.
5. Dr Joseph Wheelwright, author's interview, November 1977.

Much of the material on the early days of the Institute came from the author's interview with Dr James Witzig of Eugene, Oregon in June 1977. Dr Witzig was a member of that first class.

CHAPTER TWO

Mother

Too much has been written about the importance of the mother in infant psychology for anyone to doubt it seriously. Much evil and much good is laid in the maternal lap. In Jung's psychology the biological mother is no less important, and behind her stands the image of the primordial or archetypal mother. Jung was also particularly conscious of both figures in his own personal life. Shadows of the greater figure can be glimpsed constantly behind his mother, Emilie Preiswerk Jung. 'One [memory] recalls a slender young woman wearing a dress made of black printed all over with green crescents, who could be happy and laughing but was subject to fits of depression.'[1] This was Jung's earliest recollection of his mother and one is tempted to linger on the significance of the memory of what she was wearing, given the folklore and mythologies of the Great Mother that permeate Jungian psychology and who was so important to humanity for thousands of years prior to the patriarchal era. The crescent moons are reminiscent of the many Moon Goddesses that are found all over the world: the Egyptian Isis, Selene of the Greeks and Mona of the Celts.

It is Jung's mother who lingers in the mind after reading the semi-autobiographical work, *Memories, Dreams, Reflections*. Much further in the background is the shadowy, sad figure of a father who brooded over his religion and who felt that the best days of his life had ended when he left school. Of his mother he wrote such passages as: '. . . she was somehow rooted in the deep invisible ground, though it never appeared to me as confidence in her Christian faith. For me it was somehow connected with animals, trees, meadows, and running water, all of

8

which contrasted most strangely with her Christian faith . . . it never occurred to me how "pagan" this foundation was.'[2]

Animals, trees, meadows, and running water . . . with these images we are once again in the presence and domain of the Great Mother, rather than the Judaeo-Christian God. And Emilie keeps this pagan goddess quality throughout her son's autobiography. He refers many times to her 'second personality' ('and then her unconscious personality would put in an appearance') which spoke with the voice of a sibyl, and which was unexpectedly powerful: 'a somber imposing figure, possessed of unmistakable authority and no bones about it.'[3] This smacks of the central character in one of Jung's favourite works of fiction, *She*, by H. Rider Haggard, in which She is also a goddess-like woman who is referred to as She Who Must Be Obeyed.

'I was sure that she consisted of two personalities, one innocuous and human, the other uncanny. This other emerged only now and then, but each time it was unexpected and frightening . . . what she said struck me to the core of my being, so that I was stunned into silence.'[4] This second personality shares the qualities of the Cumaean sibyl or the Delphic oracle. The portrait evoked is that of a woman from ancient times, a mythological being. In his own writings he states that encounters with the archetypes sometimes take place in high-flown language and archaic speech.

Jung admitted to a friend of one of his biographers, Sir Laurens van der Post, just how much his mother influenced his thought and psychological formation. He stressed that his mother was very good to him and that she affected his development more than did his father.[5] Jung's secretary, Aniela Jaffé, has this to say: 'Jung had an intense, lifelong relationship to the Mother, that is the collective unconscious, its irrational imagery and symbolism . . . occasionally he referred to his mother complex in a negative way, calling it a fascination with the Eternal Feminine, but this turned out to be the prerequisite to his creative work.'[6]

Behind all the psychologising, a picture, cloudy at the edges, but clear in substance, begins to emerge of his mother and his relationship to her.

The fact that Emilie Preiswerk was the daughter of one clergyman and married to another tends to give a rather clichéd 'parson's wife' image to a woman who was obviously more complex. That, of course, is the problem with such simplifications; they rarely capture anything of the individual human being behind them.

Emilie's father, Samuel Preiswerk, was hardly a typical parson. Beside an obsession with the idea of Zion and his Hebrew studies, which seemed to interest him more than his more prosaic duties, he regularly practised psychism of a rather peculiar sort. He spoke to his deceased first wife every week at clairvoyant sessions while his second wife, Emilie's mother, looked on. It is likely that his second wife was not particularly enthralled with the idea, and this probably created a psychic atmosphere of its own.[7]

Later on, Emilie was required by her father to stand behind his chair while he worked, to protect him from ghosts or demons who might sneak up from behind. Obviously, though he trafficked with spirits, he was not altogether comfortable with them. What Emilie was supposed to do in the event of such an attack was never made clear. Perhaps her virginity was enough to keep them from putting in an appearance. Certainly her father's expectations of such invasions would make an indelible impression on the psyche of the child whether she 'saw' anything or not. Add to this the family belief that her mother was possessed of second sight and it becomes understandable why Emilie developed a second personality of an uncanny nature.

One of Jung's first papers in psychology was based on yet more psychic happenings from his mother's side of the family: his observation work with a young, mediumistic cousin. The paper was entitled 'On the Psychology and Pathology of so-called Occult Phenomena'. These experiments were conducted with Helene Preiswerk and the seances were also attended by his mother. Some time before these experiments, Jung's mother was also close by to witness two major psychic happenings. An old family table of round, solid walnut split across the top with a loud noise. And a few months later, a kitchen knife in a drawer snapped in four places with another loud noise. These occurrences obviously impressed Jung greatly as the knife is still in the family's possession.

How much of his mother's own psychism might have been due to the repressions of a vital young woman with no intellectual outlets, married to a sad dreamy man who felt that his best years were behind him, was never speculated upon by Jung, but undoubtedly it added insight in his later career to his treatment of the young women who were to come to him for help. He was aware, however, of his mother's potential gifts. He describes how ' . . . she also liked to talk and her chatter was like the gay 'plashing of a fountain. She had a decided literary gift as well as taste and depth. But this quality never properly emerged; it remained hidden beneath a semblance of a kindly old fat woman, extremely hospitable, and a possessor of a great sense of humour.'[8] This realisation of his mother's unlived potential surfaced later when he encouraged the women whom he analysed to pursue interests and careers.

The degree of sublimation of Emilie Jung's energies is indicated in the fact that at one point she had to enter a hospital for the treatment of an unspecified illness. In various biographies of Jung it has been suggested that this might have been a mental breakdown, but it need not have been so obvious. More often it is the body that breaks down in the form of a somatic complaint under the pressures and repressions of the mind, and serves up a physical illness instead that will take the place of an actual mental breakdown when façades become too much of a burden to maintain. Jung was evidently marked by this absence as he makes clear when he recollects eighty years later. 'I was deeply troubled by my mother's being away. From then on, I was always mistrustful when the word "love" was spoken.'[9] And, one wonders, 'woman' as well?

He continued to associate his mother with paganism

rather than with the Christian faith until her death when he was forty-seven, in 1922. On the night of her death he had a dream which was rooted in Teutonic mythology. 'It was a heroic primeval landscape. Suddenly I heard a piercing whistle that seemed to resound through the whole universe. My knees shook. . . . A gigantic wolfhound with a fearful, gaping maw burst forth. At the sight of it, the blood froze in my veins. It tore past me and I suddenly knew: the Wild Huntsman had commanded it to carry away a human soul. I awoke in deadly terror, and the next morning I received news of my mother's passing.'[10] He goes on to interpret the dream. 'Thus the dream says that the soul of my mother was taken into that greater territory of the Self which lies beyond the segment of Christian morality.'

Undoubtedly, it was this strong relationship with his mother, and through her to the archetypal feminine, which coloured all his future relationships with women and determined his expectations of them.

Notes

1. V. Brome, *Jung; Man and Myth.*
2. C.G. Jung, *Memories, Dreams, Reflections.*
3. Ibid.
4. Ibid.
5. Sir Laurens van der Post, *Jung and the Story of our Time.*
6. A. Jaffe, *The Life and Work of C.G. Jung.*
7. V. Brome, *Jung; Man and Myth.*
8. C.G. Jung, *Memories, Dreams, Reflections.*
9. Ibid.
10. Ibid.

CHAPTER THREE

The Beginnings of the Entourage

'The Valkyries are also called Wish-Maidens; and now and then, one of them becomes, as Brunhilde did, the wife or lover of a great hero to whom she can give help and protection in battle.'[1] This excerpt, from the only written work to be completed by Emma Jung, might well be a description of how she saw her role as wife to C.G. Jung. That there was love between them is not in question. But throughout their marriage it was Emma who was the 'rock'. She certainly tried to give help in at least one of Jung's crises, the break with Freud. In the increasingly formal letters, flying back and forth between Zurich and Vienna, it is those of Emma that have the voice of reason and indicate that she was the one who saw most clearly what was happening between her husband and his former mentor and father-figure. Throughout her life and his, it was she who tried to smooth his way, sometimes even financially, and keep things in equilibrium for him.

Very early in their married life, in letters soliciting advice from Freud,[2] she describes how she had to speak stupidly in public to make sure that no one would think that she was trying to compete with Jung. However great her love – which appears to have been intense – it must have been galling for a woman of her intellectual gifts to stifle her power in the presence of others, particularly the many women who had begun to arrive from all over the world to analyse with him. One wonders where such a mandate was born. Did it come from her own deep-seated convictions about marriage and a woman's role in it? Had Jung himself given her the idea that he wanted no

interference from her on an intellectual level? Since there
are no signs that he was afraid of intellectual competition,
this seems unlikely. Once she had decided on her role of
wife to the great man and bearer of his children (they
came with astonishing regularity from the first year of
their marriage), perhaps she feared to step into unknown
territory.

By the year 1911, when she had written the first of a
series of confidential letters to Freud, Toni Wolff, her only
serious rival of whom we are aware, had already been on
the scene for a year. It was around this time that both
women attended the Weimar Conference with Jung, and
it may have been then that Emma realised that her
greatest chance of maintaining her marriage lay in not
attempting to compete with Toni Wolff and the others.
She perhaps took refuge in her role, essential to Jung, of
wife-mother-container. In his autobiography Jung writes
of the critical part of his life when he was wrestling with
the unconscious. 'It was most essential for me to have a
normal life in the real world as a counterpoint to that
strange inner world. My family and my profession
remained the base to which I would always return, assur-
ing me that I was an actually existing person. But my
family and the knowledge: I have a medical diploma from
a Swiss university; I must help my patients; I have a wife
and five children; I live at 228 Seestrasse in Kusnacht –
these were actualities which made demands on me and
proved to me again and again that I really existed, that
I was not a blank page whirling about in the winds of
the spirit like Nietzsche. Thus my family and my
profession always remained a joyful reality and *a guarantee
that I also had a normal existence* [italics mine].'[3] Perhaps
Emma Jung realised his very strong need for such
normality in the face of what he had set out to explore
and decided, not without ambivalence, to provide just
that for him.

Emma Rauchenbach was the daughter of a wealthy
industrialist from an old Swiss family. There are a few
stories to the effect that Jung first met her when she was
fourteen (another source says fifteen and still another,

sixteen), and that he told a friend who was with him at the time that she was going to be his wife. A pretty story, but things were not to be quite so simple, because Emma refused him once before accepting his second proposal. There are hints from other sources of a stormier prenuptial relationship with its ups and downs.

While Emma was still a young girl, family tragedy struck in the form of her father's blindness, which made him become very bitter. This, for some reason, resulted in Emma being prevented from going on to college. By the time Jung came to court her, his intellectual brilliance must have stirred her imagination and might conceivably have provided her with the stimulus she herself had been denied.

Within a year of their marriage, she had her first child, and was to have four more children by the time they had been married for eleven years. Her letters to Freud preceded the birth of her fourth child. So did the advent of Toni Wolff. In those days, the appearance of another woman was not unusual in a conventional marriage. What was unusual was that as time went on, the triangle was acknowledged by the three people concerned, and an attempt was made to live with it, to the point where Jung spent Wednesdays with Toni and she came to dinner at the house on Sundays. The attempt was at least outwardly successful, and lasted until the death of Fräulein Wolff in 1953.

The pain experienced by all three people was evident to all those around them, and is guardedly expressed by sympathetic biographers of Jung. 'Of course there were the most painful difficulties for everyone concerned, especially before a *modus vivendi* was reached.'[4] But the 'dignity and willingness with which she [Toni Wolff] accepted this role and the apparent ease with which she ignored the world jealous of her special relationship with Jung, should not be allowed to disguise the staggering burdens it imposed upon her.'[5] Of course, it might be argued that Toni Wolff accepted it the easiest of the three because it gave her a special privilege to be privy to all the thoughts and information coming from the man whom she undoubtedly held in highest regard. However, '. . . they observed Toni Wolff repeatedly in the grip of great distress'.[6] Van der Post goes on to tell us how at Bollingen Tower, built along the lines of the miniature stone houses Jung built as a child, one stone is carved to Emma, referring to her as 'the foundation of the house', while another is carved for Toni Wolff, 'the fragrance of the house'. One wonders if Emma might have preferred being the fragrance. There is something very maternal about being the foundation. What really went on in the hearts of those three people we will never know now that the letters are burnt and the people dead. But perhaps the best statement of Emma's feelings about her dilemma is contained in a letter to Freud dated 24 November 1911:[7] 'The women are naturally all in love with him. . . . Carl says I should no longer concentrate as before only on him and the children, but what on earth am I to do?' This letter poses a question that would be a difficult one to answer even in these liberated days for a woman who had hitherto devoted her energies to the family and suddenly finds herself no longer the chief object of her husband's attentions. Consider how much more devastating such a position must have been in the early part of this century. Jung seems at times to have been quite able to formulate things in such a way as to free himself and his conscience while appearing liberal for the age in which he lived.

Emma turned to analytical work as she began to have more free time. One of her first patients, who was receiving analysis from Jung, was sent to her because she dreamed that Emma had something for her. This was the beginning of a pattern that continued throughout the years between Toni, Emma and Jung: many people had analysis with at least two of them.

People who knew her during these years have said that Emma seemed like a fulfilled woman who enjoyed her career and who brooked no nonsense from Jung. Since these observations were made from outside the triangle there is no way to know how accurate they are. Many apparently 'happy' marriages break up every day.

According to at least one observer, Emma had a sense

of humour when dealing with her husband and was not in awe of him. Once, at dinner, someone asked Jung why he did not deal with children. He replied that they did not interest him as they didn't have much symbolic material. Emma commented, 'Oh, Carl, No one interests you who doesn't have much symbolic material!' There were many occasions when she deflated him if he became too pompous. According to Dr Michael Fordham[8] she often aimed a well-placed kick under the table at Jung when he made some outrageous or pompous remark.

She did not embark on her large work on the Grail until after her children were well on their way to growing up. Her first work was published in 1931, twenty-seven years after her marriage, on the concept of the animus, from a lecture which she gave at the Zurich Psychological Club. The Grail book was still unfinished at her death and was only published after Marie-Louise von Franz had completed it at Jung's request.

As is common in many marriages, Emma came for Jung to be associated with the image of the mother and wife, the very foundation of the family, and we shall never know whether this caused her sadness and stress, or whether she merely accepted it as her 'lot'. Many men find it expedient after years of marriage to relate to their wives mainly as the mother to their children, and in some way become emotional children to the wife. Sometimes the wife is so caught up in the rigours of caring for children and home that she is not aware of the mental or emotional defection of her husband until it is too late. There is a suggestion, from someone who had a brief friendship with Jung near the end of his life, that something like this may have happened in Jung's own marriage.

Jung is reported to have said to Miguel Serrano[9] that 'In my long psychiatric experience, I never came across a marriage that was entirely self-sufficient. . . . ideally the man should contain the woman and remain outside her.' Jung told Freud he was suffering from the 'nuptual complex' and said finally, 'The prerequisite for a good marriage, it seems to me is the license to be unfaithful.'[10] . . . 'I think the French have found the solution in the

Number Three. Frequently this number occurs in magic marriages. ... '[11] This seems to have been true in the Jungs' marriage: Number Three came in the person of Toni Wolff.

The death of Emma Jung in 1955 shook the foundations of Jung's life and he never totally recovered from it. In old age, he had turned to his wife more and more, and the relationship with Toni, according to Ruth Bailey[13] had become somewhat of a burden. Emma's death affected him more profoundly than when Toni had died a few years before. He obviously felt that with Emma's passing the 'help and protection in battle' had been withdrawn, never to be replaced.

Notes

1. E. Jung, *Animus and Anima*.
2. McGuire (ed.), *The Freud/Jung Letters*.
3. C.G. Jung, *Memories, Dreams, Reflections*.
4. B. Hannah, *Jung: His Life and Work*.
5. Sir L. van der Post, *Jung and the Story of Our Time*.
6. Ibid.
7. McGuire (ed.) *The Freud/Jung Letters*.
8. Dr Michael Fordham, author's interview, January 1979.
9. M. Schocken and M. Serrano, *C.G. Jung and Hermann Hesse: A Record of Two Friendships*.
10. L. Donn, *Freud and Jung: Years of Friendship, Years of Loss*.
11. M. Schocken and M. Serrano, *C.G. Jung and Hermann Hesse: A Record of Two Friendships*.
12. V. Brome, *Jung, Man and Myth*.

CHAPTER FOUR

The Early Circle

Jung's career got into full swing in the years preceding the First World War and, from the beginning, most of his patients were drawn from the many foreigners filling Zurich at that time. His international reputation had begun to spread as a result of his association with Freud and his subsequent trip to Clark University in the United States to lecture on his work with the Word Association Test. One of the clients he attracted to him at that time was to have a great effect on the course of his work. He was Harold McCormick, whose wife, Edith, was the daughter of John D. Rockefeller.

Zurich was, in those pre-war days, a virtual alchemist's oven in which varied and disparate ingredients resulted in some remarkable ideas. It was a focal point of expatriate activity where ideas crystallised which would influence cultural and even political trends all over the world for the next few decades. Artists, writers, and politicians were running up against one another in ways which produced revolutionary ideas and associations. From Germany and Eastern Europe came a handful of emigrés who met together and produced the Dada movement in art and literature. Hugo Ball, Tristan Tzara, Hans Richter and others met nightly in the Café Odeon, the hub of café life which was to continue throughout the war. It was there that Ball conceived the idea of the Café Voltaire, which became the focal point and showcase of the Dada group in the Spiegelgasse in the Altstadt section of the city. Proclamations were issued nightly from its stage, which was also the scene of activities which outraged the bourgeois Swiss.

Just up the street, Lenin lived and waited with his

associates for a word from Russia. It is unlikely that such a serious man would have ever come into the Café Voltaire owing to its notoriety and its outrageous activities, yet surely its atmosphere of revolution would not have seemed inimical to him. Not far away, James Joyce was drinking and holding forth at the Odeon one night and the Pfauenstube the next, writing *Ulysses* during the day.

Zurich was the tense and often claustrophobic dead centre of the war in Europe. It was a virtual container, neatly sealed off and protected from all the turmoil that was taking place in the rest of the world. In his diaries, Hugo Ball described Switzerland, and by extension, Zurich, as a 'bird cage, surrounded by roaring lions'. But it was that very atmosphere of heightened living and experience that provided the soil necessary for such a cultural flowering.

Into this setting came Edith Rockefeller McCormick who saw Jung, as did her husband Harold, for therapy. It has been said that she first tried to lure Jung to the United States, offering him and his family a luxurious home. Jung refused, telling her that she must come to Switzerland if she wished to see him. She did. It was a rushed trip of Jung's to McCormick that almost resulted in him missing the famous Weimar Congress (a meeting of various psycho-analytic associations, headed by Freud).

From all contemporary accounts, Mrs McCormick was a rather capricious woman who felt that her wealth would buy her anything, who fancied herself in the role of patroness of the arts and who for a while endowed Joyce until, in a customarily abrupt manner, and without warning (although friends of his had warned him from experience of previous dealings with her), she withdrew her patronage. Jung said later that it was possible, although he didn't recollect it, that he counselled her to do this. He had given similar advice in the case of another artist supported by Mrs McCormick who had run into a 'dry spell' in his creativity. Afterwards he had felt his judgement vindicated by the fact that the man had gone from that long dry period into a time of full production. Jung had a theory that Mrs McCormick's patronage sometimes sapped the artist's will to create. Presumably he didn't feel that starvation of self and family might also hinder the creative process.

Jung's only knowledge of Joyce was through his consultations with Mrs McCormick. She had probably told Jung that she believed that Joyce drank and kept late hours, but had not added that he still put in a full day's productive work. Perhaps Jung felt such a subsidy would only encourage such behaviour and keep Joyce from serious writing. Whatever the reasons, it is unlikely, given Mrs McCormick's own character, that Jung's counsel alone caused the severance of support. She was well known for her whims in bestowing and withdrawing her financial gifts.

Another, more plausible possibility is that when Joyce declined Mrs McCormick's advice that he should have some analysis with Jung she let the well of her benificence dry up in retaliation. The fact remains that Joyce held Jung responsible and wrote the following letter, which summed up his feelings: ' . . . a batch of people in Zurich persuaded themselves that I was gradually going mad and actually endeavoured to induce me to enter a sanitorium where a certain Dr Jung (the Swiss Tweedledum who is not to be confused with the Viennese Tweedledee, Dr Freud) amuses himself at the expense (in every sense of the word) of ladies and gentlemen who are troubled with bees in their bonnets.'[2]

Jung's relationship with Mrs McCormick continued for several years and he benefited greatly from her in a financial way. She was in Zurich with her husband from 1913 to 1923, being analysed by him, then herself doing some work as an analyst and studying philosophy. She was very much a 'grande dame' and Joyce did an amusing, if malicious sketch of her as Mrs Mervin Talboys in the *Circe* episode in *Ulysses*. In this, she is portrayed as an exaggerated sort of sadistic society queen sporting a riding crop. Earlier, he had tried to get her to appear in his play, *Exiles*, in which he thought that her fashionable clothes, jewels and furs would make her just right for a role he had in mind. She declined to appear.

Her major subsidy to Jung was in the form of the purchase of what was to become the central meeting place for his circle and the venue of his psychological dissertations: the Zurich Psychological Club. In keeping with her role as an American society leader, it started out on a very grand scale. Too grand, as it turned out, for few of the members could afford the accommodation or the dining room. The property was located in one of the most expensive areas in Zurich, but eventually moved to more modest headquarters on the Gemeindestrasse, where it remained until the late 1970s. It is now in the Kusnacht. The second floor of this building is rented out to the C.G. Jung Institute, which also occupied a similar position in the previous building, since the Second World War.

The Club opened with a great fanfare on 26 February 1916, with forty people present including Emma Jung, Toni Wolff and others. Emma was the Club's first president, followed by Toni.

The importance of the Club to Jung and the women around him cannot be overemphasised. First of all, as has been previously stated, many of Jung's patients were foreigners. The Swiss in general are an insular people, self-absorbed and wary of non-Swiss. In terms of Jung's psychological types (which he himself applied to nations), the Swiss are an extremely introverted society. They look with suspicion on the new, the different, and particularly the foreign. This is as true today as it was then. Unfortunately, unlike many other countries in Europe where expatriates can form ties in a short period of time with the citizens of the host country, in Switzerland this process takes many, many years, if indeed it ever really happens. The language also provides one of the major difficulties as it is not properly a language at all but a dialect which only very recently was given a published guide. It is called Schweizer-Deutsch and is supposedly a bastardisation of High German, but doesn't sound like it at all. Consequently, if a foreigner does not happen across a grocer or concierge who speaks his language, he is apt to remain only able to speak to his analyst. Speaking knowledge of High German is of little use outside the classroom with any but the most educated. One's German might be understood, but not the reply in dialect! The myth of the tri-lingual Swiss is a travel agent's dream which only materialises in the finest shops, hotels and restaurants.

It is to Jung's credit that he was aware of all this and sympathised with the plight of his patients and students. Not only were they plunging into uncharted regions of the human psyche, but they were thrown into a culture which, if not overtly hostile, was distinctly cool toward them. He had been concerned for some time about this problem, and the Club and Mrs McCormick's backing of it seemed like a good solution.

Once the Club was able to get past that lady's grandiose ideas (which stemmed perhaps from her membership of posh American social clubs), it did provide another source of support for his English-speaking followers. Coming so soon after his break with Freud, it also provided a measure of support for Jung himself. It must have been comforting for him to have his own circle of literate, interested people, eager to grasp his ideas as they poured forth from him. Later, the English seminars were to provide another place of refuge for his English-speaking followers.

The Club also became the place where the various analysands and analysts of the Jungian persuasion could come together and find kindred souls in a world when the search for self-knowledge was still not widespread. Today, with our Esalens, ESTs, and metaphysical centres, not to mention the innumerable ashrams that proliferated during the 1960s, 1970s and 1980s, it is hard to imagine how 'ivory-tower' this must have all seemed to the world at large. It is no coincidence that the early circle was made up mainly of the well-educated, wealthy upper classes and the art world. It is also no coincidence that the circle started up so soon after the break with Freud, when Jung was isolated from so many of his colleagues who had broken with him. From the beginning, Jung used the Club as a place to discuss with his own circle the material with which he was currently working. In this way, it provided a sounding board and place where he could break in his new ideas.

Inevitably there were rituals. For one thing, there were the chairs. Several were labelled with the names of the more prominent members: 'Frau Jung', 'Fräulein Wolff', 'Professor Jung', and so on. If ever the people to whom these chairs were assigned were not present, they remained empty. One woman, present at the early meetings, claimed that a numinous feeling hovered around each chair.

There was also an ice-breaking ritual, which took the form of a game known as 'alleluia'. This game simply involved tossing a handkerchief to someone, who caught it and tossed it to someone else. The handkerchief or napkin was knotted to give it weight. Since the ladies in the Club as a rule dressed very elegantly and the gentlemen were always in dress suits, collars and ties, it is amusing to think of them playing such a game and little wonder that it took them out of their personas and lessened the formalities. Jung always had a genius for such ideas.

If there was a feeling of cult at the Club, there was also sometimes the sense of its being a battleground. Jung's circle always prided themselves on the acceptance of their own shadows, or hidden selves. The result of this at the Club was that when they were angry they let it be known, and when they were jealous they let that be known too. While this must have been refreshing in such a conventional society, it made for some 'hot times' at the Club. It was the jealousy that most often came to the surface. Used to having Jung to themselves during their analytical hour, some found it difficult to share him at the Club. This may be the source of Toni Wolff's legendary aloofness. As Jung's half-acknowledged mistress, she must have felt the currents of jealousy swirling around. It went largely unexpressed possibly for fear of arousing Jung's own temper which was well-known and periodically demonstrated at the Club.

Early on, there was a conflict of such proportions as to drive Jung away for a time. This involved the women, a couple of men within the Club and Jung himself. Reports vary as to whether Jung, his wife and Toni Wolff all walked out, or just Jung. Either way, Jung was not there for a time and this could have been due as much to his need to be by himself as to any fight. When one thinks of his long analytical hours, it seems almost heroic that he should have chosen to spend any extra time at all with patients. In fact, in most other schools of psychology, the analyst avoids spending any social time whatsoever with patients. His own needs must also have been great. He also had the demands of a growing family, even though Emma took the lion's share of the responsibility on herself.

Although the periphery was always changing, there was a core group that remained constant throughout the years. Two of this inner circle were Swiss: Antonia 'Toni' Wolff and Linda Fierz-David.

Notes

1. R. Huelsenbeck, *Memoirs of a Dada Drummer*.
2. Brady (ed.), *Letters of James Joyce*.
3. Ibid.
4. Ibid.
5. Hilde Kirsch, author's interview, February 1978.

CHAPTER FIVE

The Fragrance

If the names of some of the Jungian women draw ambivalent responses from surviving contemporaries, that of Antonia (Toni) Wolff evokes either complete silence or a guarded appreciation of her role as Jung's assistant. At no time does one hear the word 'mistress' from anyone. Yet that, quite simply or perhaps not so simply, was her role. She became his collaborator and did some independent work on his psychology. The fact remains that her chief involvement with Jung, at least in its beginnings, was as the 'other woman' in a whispered, but much discussed, triangle. This triangle of Jung, Emma and Toni has been alternately praised for its openness (Emma was aware of the relationship, perhaps from the start), and deplored for the pain which it inflicted on both women. More rarely, the question is asked why Jung insisted on such a relationship continuing in view of the obvious pain it caused his wife. The fact remains that he did. Toni has been referred to as Jung's 'femme inspiratrice', 'soror mystica' or 'anima', which translate into English as 'inspiring woman' or muse, 'mystical sister' in the alchemical opuses, and 'soul'. They all sound quite high-flown and more like the official titles that reigning monarchs bestow on their lovers, or terms that poets use to describe important relationships with women, usually mistresses, seldom wives. There is no indication that Jung himself used any of them to his credit. They imply a transcendence of the physical realm into the spiritual. This was certainly the case with Jung and Fräulein Wolff, who was not only analysed by, but who also analysed, her mentor. The terms were used by his followers possibly to avoid the negative publicity which would have emerged if Jung had

26

been known to have a mistress. Sounding rather arch at best and kittenish at the worst, they continue to be used in recent biographies of Jung. In the course of interviews for this book I was often told that his relationship with Toni was 'different', a term often applied to such relationships as an excuse. It does not seem to occur to the people who employ these terms and explanations that they are no longer necessary. The revelation simply serves to show that Jung was as human as many people before him and since.

Toni Wolff was born in 1888, thirteen years after Jung. She was also, like him, a native-born Swiss. Her father, whom she adored, was an aristocrat and a successful business man, twenty years older than his wife. He had an affinity for Japan, where he often travelled, and there were even rumours that he had Japanese blood which gave him his 'foreign' good looks. Toni, too, had something exotic in her dark, brooding beauty; something un-Swiss. Someone once described Toni as a black pearl and Jung agreed with this description.[1]

Soon after Toni was born the family moved to the house where she was to live until her mother died sixty years later. Even then she only moved next door. There was apparently never any break in the continuity of family ties for Toni.

It was this intensity of ties that brought her into Jung's consulting room in 1910. A year earlier, her father had set out one day for his club as usual. Once there, he died suddenly. This death, combined with some difficulties with her mother, resulted in Toni having a serious nervous breakdown at the age of twenty-one. The following year, having had little success with other doctors, Frau Wolff brought her daughter to Jung whose reputation was just beginning to spread. Several of Jung's associates have speculated that Toni Wolff was the case referred to as Jung's one cure of schizophrenia. If this is true, it might be that his own subsequent 'descent into the unconscious' had more than a little to do with the contamination that can take place within an analyst when working with a schizophrenic patient. This occurs when a specific illness being treated meets the unconscious working out of similar problems in the psyche of the analyst.

At this time, Toni was a dark, intense-looking woman who was just beginning to project the rather forbidding persona which she may have developed to protect her very vulnerable nature which had been placed in a trying situation. She was a good example of the aristocratic young Swiss woman, cultured by birth, but conventionally educated without a serious thought as to vocation. She had written poetry at the university which was praised by her professors, but she did not regard herself as a poet. In other words, she was gifted and intelligent, but had no proper outlet for it. Whatever the clinical diagnosis of her breakdown, this was most probably one of the contributing causes.

This, then was the young woman who appeared in Jung's life during one of its critical phases: approaching middle age. Jung was thirty-five, and he had already been married seven years. Within a year of beginning her analysis, she was invited by Jung to the conference at Weimar, along with his wife. Jung wrote a letter to Freud beforehand, describing 'Fräulein Antonia Wolff, a remarkable intellect with an excellent feeling for religion and philosophy.'[2] She appears in a much-published picture taken at Weimar in 1911, discreetly separated from Jung and Emma by another woman. She is wide-eyed, intense, and questioning.

By 1911, Emma needed an analytical confidant and began to correspond with Freud, discussing the strains on her marriage. Jung was not aware of this correspondence until it ended. Among her complaints were the many women who gathered around her husband, 'while with the men I am constantly cordoned off as the wife of the father or friend.'[3] Any guessing as to the date when the relationship between Jung and Toni began slipping beyond that of doctor/patient are futile. It is as good a guess as any that it was most probably just after the break with Freud was final, in 1913. This date would have coincided with the end of Toni's therapy which Jung once told a friend had lasted three years. After the break with

Freud, Jung felt cast adrift and friendless. He felt he was putting his chosen profession in jeopardy, and psychologically speaking, that he was committing parricide. (Freud had once interpreted one of Jung's dreams to mean that Jung had an unconscious desire to kill him.) Jung was beginning one of the most tortuous periods of his life. His fantasies took on a peculiar half-life of their own which made him fear for his sanity. In fact, he states in his autobiography that 'in the drawer of my night table lay a loaded revolver and I became frightened'[4] – so that if he felt he was being taken over by his own psychological material he could take his life and spare his family.

One of the first fantasies which appeared to him was a vision of the ill-assorted couple Salome and Elijah, the young woman and the old prophet. Jung has recorded how he questioned the phantom figure as to the appropriateness of the pairing. To this the old man replied that 'they had been together throughout all eternity'. Perhaps this was his psyche's way of giving meaning to the troubling relationship that was developing between himself and Toni. Again, in *Memories, Dreams, Reflections*, he states, 'But of those relationships which *were vital to me and which came to me like memories of far-off times*, I cannot speak, for they pertain not only to my innermost life, but that of others. It is not for me to open to the public eye doors that are closed for ever.'[5]

For it was to Toni that he turned as he began his descent into the dark, largely unexplored realms of the mind. Emma had her hands full with five children and the mechanics of what contemporaries have described as a beautifully run household. She was the rock after all, the foundation, and it was possible that Jung did not want her to accompany him in this dangerous undertaking for fear he might infect *her*. Emma was to say, many years later when Toni died, 'I shall always be grateful to her for doing for my husband what I or anyone else could not have done at a most critical time.'[6]

Just what she did, we can only guess from similar experiences in Jungian analysis. In the first place, she must have done a great deal of listening. And she would have had to be non-judgemental in attitude. In essence, she had to become his analyst. When one is describing the dreams and fantasies which arise in archaic, peculiar and often ridiculous form, it is important that the listener does not interpret because this will often interrupt the natural flow of images. The material of fantasy is so close to the wanderings of the mind in schizophrenic breaks as to be almost indistinguishable. This occurs when the material from the unconscious comes into consciousness in the form of visions and images which are uncontrolled. It is the source of the psychiatric term 'acute schizophrenia' which is much more easily treated than paranoid schizophrenia. There must not be any overt or even subliminal message to the person involved that the symbols are 'crazy' or 'stupid', for that is often what the person fears. By his own admission, Jung feared this. The images must be treated as 'real', but not worried in the way a cat worries a mouse. Toni, with her poet's sensibilities, was most likely able to take these images and treat them as metaphors, and research them in the literature of the then young sciences of anthropology and folklore. When a dream symbol seems particularly strange or worrisome, this is sometimes the best medicine: to find the symbol as it connects to past myths.

With Toni both physically and emotionally so close, able to devote her time to him in a way which a woman with a household to run could not, there must have also been a degree of ambivalence. It is interesting to speculate that the severity of his struggle, which she helped to ease, might have in some way been intensified by the complications that such a relationship brought to his life. There is no doubt that he loved Emma and felt her central to his life, and so it is hardly likely that he would have started another intense relationship without inner turmoil.

Whatever the agonies that Jung suffered, the complications must have been worse for Toni. For while in England and a few other European countries there has always been a niche for the unmarried woman, albeit a rather narrow one, no such niche existed in Swiss culture. Marriage was the suitable role for women there. Then there was the added difficulty of loving a married man and a prominent one at that. One begins to see what were the stresses for her. 'A friend who knew Toni well said of Jung, "One can say that he was a big spoon – he drank her soul".'[7] One of her former patients has written that an American friend of hers who was in Zurich in the early 1920s and 1930s, said of Toni's equivocal position as mistress to Jung, 'My God, she was courageous. She just *made* them accept it.'[8] 'Them' of course referred to the Jungian group and most particularly the other women within it. It is doubtful that anyone outside that élite group would have found it acceptable. In this early part of the century, the full effects of Victorian decorum were still being felt, particularly in Switzerland, which had until recently a law against 'adulterous meetings' and where only in the last thirty years have women had the right to vote.

Something which aided the acceptance of the relationship was that quality of Toni's which many have mentioned: her spinsterish, forbidding air. Someone in the Inner Circle remarked that 'Toni was all spirit. It was almost as if she *had* no body.'[9] Perhaps this kept enough people from being certain about the exact nature of their relationship. Jolande Jacobi maintained that Jung was undersexed, but this is generally thought to have been jealousy on her part. To this day, however, there are Jungians from that time who wonder out loud if anything physical between Jung and Toni ever took place. In view of the pain caused Emma and Toni, however, this view seems hardly worthy of consideration.

Toni became his assistant, and her duties seem to have been concerned mainly with research into the imagery emerging from his own encounters with the unconscious, which he later called the 'prima materia' for all his future thought and work. Many of the women who became his assistants in the following years also performed these tasks for him. In addition, she often accompanied him on his increasingly frequent trips abroad, Emma often coming along too. On one of these trips to the Tavistock lectures in England, Toni brought such a number of hat boxes that an observer was sure that she had a hat for each day. She dressed like a Parisienne in 'well-cut dresses, her hair always beautifully done, waved back from her forehead. Very elegant. . . .'[10]

On another trip, to the Ravenna mosaics, Jung and Toni had an experience that can only be described as a joint vision, showing how strong the psychic link was between them. As they went into the piscina, they walked through a blue, misty light through which some mosaics became visible. They were there for half an hour, looking at them and discussing what they saw. They saw Peter being saved by Christ after having attempted to walk on the water, and others, including Moses bringing forth water from the rock, and Jonah and the whale.

Upon their return to Zurich, Jung shared with his students their experience with the mosaics. When a colleague announced a couple of years later that he was going, Jung asked him to take pictures of the mosaics as he and Toni had failed to photograph them. When the man returned from his trip, he told Jung there were no such mosaics. Jung was stunned. He and Toni had seen them with their own eyes. Later, after much research, they learned that the Empress Galla Placida had made a vow during a terrible winter boat crossing that if she survived she would have several mosaics created. She did indeed survive, had the mosaics created, and built the Basilica of San Giovanni to house them. Then, *in the early Middle Ages the church and the mosaics were destroyed completely.* Jung and Toni had 'seen' mosaics that had been gone for several hundred years!

Inevitably, Toni began to wish to be an analyst. Jung tried to discourage her, ostensibly because he felt that her literary gifts would not find sufficient time for expression. (At one time he compared her poetry to Goethe's.) Possibly he might have also been reluctant because he did not wish to engage in 'shop talk' with her. A *femme inspiratrice* engaged in the same profession might cease to be inspiring or restful. By 1929, however, he seems to have accepted the inevitable, and at the same time urged her to become president of the Zurich Psychological Club. Their relationship was now in its sixteenth year and perhaps he felt she needed to concern herself with matters other than him. Possibly he himself was tiring of such a complicated relationship.

She became the 'tiger' of the Club, trying to maintain the number of members with whom Jung would feel at home, and keeping an eye on everything so that Jung would not be bothered by anyone or anything that did not interest him. Several members of the Club commented on her intuitive awareness, amounting to psychism, of the atmosphere around Jung. Today we might call it 'co-dependency' which can be seen as doing things for another person on a regular basis that they could do for themselves, and being more attuned to their needs, desires and feelings than one is to one's own.

Her confidence grew, although she never felt entirely happy in groups. Dr Joseph Henderson has commented that of all the people around Jung, Toni, Linda Fierz-David and Emma 'kept their shape best'. She was very much herself then, and would not be bullied by him. In fact, she developed a knack of putting him in his place when he became inflated with his own self-importance. It was a knack which she shared with Fierz-David and Emma.

She was not, however, at home with women. Aside from Linda Fierz-David with whom she was close, she doesn't seem to have had any women friends. Every woman with whom I spoke described her as intense, intelligent, beautiful, but not one of them spoke warmly of her. One woman analyst said, 'If you were a woman she had to lord it over you. If you were a man, it was peaches and cream. I didn't get along with her, I put up with her. But I *did* work with her.' Dr Joseph Wheelwright said simply, 'Toni was the best analyst I ever had; better than Jung in my estimation.'[11]

Mary Bancroft writes, 'I considered Toni Wolff highly intelligent with a cultured background that impressed me deeply. But I also found her personality so unpleasant that I knew I'd pay strict attention to the matter at hand [analysis] so as to finish it as soon as possible. One day she told me that working with me was like wrestling with a boa constrictor.'[12] She was infuriated when Bancroft laughed.

Possibly she felt that any woman who showed up in Zurich to work with Jung was a potential rival for his affections. As one source has said, '. . . but on one point their recollections reliably converged: Jung's effect on women was overwhelming'.[13] Certainly most of the women, as well as his female clients, were in love with him, at least a little. The transference was no doubt felt by him as a burden, but could have still been painful for Toni in her special position. And Jung *did* enjoy the attentions of women. It was said that in his later years he could always be found with the youngest and prettiest women in any gathering and most often they were Americans.

One woman who was analysed by Toni had a different picture of her. 'She sat at a long, flat-topped desk, and you sat, not across from her, but at her side. She used to sit there like a little queen and smoke . . . with a long black cigarette holder. She had a deep voice. . . . She was like a mother to me.' The same woman goes on to recount how, when she was going home to America, her husband met Toni Wolff on the street and told her that his wife was 'frightened to death, in a terrible panic' over having to travel by plane. And Toni replied very quietly: 'Tell her that I don't think that the plane will fall down.'[14]

After Jung built Bollingen Tower, he and Toni would often spend quiet weekends there. At first, she did not appreciate the fact that there was neither running water nor electricity, but soon she enjoyed it as much as he did and looked forward to their times there. Emma never spent much time at Bollingen.

In describing Toni's personality and appearance, it is easy to forget one important fact: her real contribution to the body of Jungian knowledge. Until recently her work has suffered from lack of translation, and so has not had an audience outside of analytical psychology trainees and teachers. Most of the material she has written is to be found only in the files of the libraries of the various C.G.

Jung Institutes around the world. In 1978, Dr C.A. Meier spoke of the books being published in Switzerland but none have yet appeared in English.

One of the earliest known pieces she wrote is entitled *The Structures of the Feminine Psyche*, which though using the Jungian concept of psychological types as a base, is very much her own work and thought. A valuable work it is, showing a perceptive intuition about the roles women assume in relation to men. However it says little about women's psychology when *not* in relationship to men, showing a very patriarchal bias. It is unfortunate that her duties as an analyst and Club president should have kept her from doing more writing. Allowed more time, her work might have developed further.

As the years went on, her relationship to Jung and to Emma stabilised and contemporary memoirs frequently state: 'Jung, Toni and Emma did such and such. . . . ' or 'Jung, Toni and Emma went to such and such. . . . ' Part of the reason why they were able to make it work as well as it did was due to the heroic efforts of both the women. At one point they both went into analysis with Dr C.A. Meier. Perhaps it was the realisation on both their parts that neither of them wished to lose Jung that helped them adjust to, and endure, such a painful situation. The triangle continued, though in greatly attenuated form, until Toni's sudden death, in 1953.

Jung was shocked by its suddenness, as she had been by the death of her father. Shortly afterwards, on Easter eve, he had a dream about her. She appeared, young and beautiful, taller than in real life, wearing a dress coloured with the hues of a bird of paradise with kingfisher blue emphasised. In Jung's first fantasies, the figure of Philemon, who evolved from Elijah, appeared to Jung with the wings of a kingfisher.[15] Jung had in this dream at last clothed Toni with the colours of the wise old man of whom she was the natural consort.[16] She had merged with him, as it were. Perhaps he was unconsciously aware that in ancient China, the kingfisher was the symbol of fidelity and mated happiness.

He carved a small stone with an enigmatic message for

her in the shadow of the trees at Kusnacht. In Chinese characters it states: 'Tony Wolff. Lotus. Nun. Mysterious.' An epitaph for an anima indeed.

It is somehow apt that Toni's death was attributed to hitherto undisclosed problems of the heart.

Notes

1. L. Down, *Freud and Jung: Years of Friendship, Years of Loss.*
2. McGuire (ed.), *The Freud/Jung Letters.*
3. Ibid.
4. B. Hannah, *Jung: His Life and Work.*
5. C.G. Jung, *Memories, Dreams, Reflections.*
6. B. Hannah, *Jung: His Life and Work.*
7. L. Down, *Freud and Jung: Years of Friendship, Years of Loss.*
8. Interview by the author, November 1976.
9. L. Down, *Freud and Jung: Years of Friendship, Years of Loss.*
10. Dr Joseph Henderson, author's interview, November 1976.
11. Dr Joseph Wheelwright, author's interview, November 1976.
12. M. Bancroft, *Psychological Perspectives*, Autumn 1975, 'Jung and his Circle'.
13. L. Down, *Freud and Jung: Years of Friendship, Years of Loss.*
14. R. Lane, *A Well of Living Water*, 'Recollections of Toni Wolff', a festschrift book, privately printed for Hilde Kirsch's 75th birthday.
15. Ibid.
16. M. Harding, *Woman's Mysteries.*

CHAPTER SIX

Sieglinde

'That is woman: dancing naked and free, then suffering and in tears, then mothering what is suffering and then being an elegant woman of the world. And the whole thing inspired by a god-like animus. Perhaps a woman comes to herself by suffering.'

These words might make the perfect epitaph for Linda Fierz-David. They were spoken by her son as he described one of the frescoes at Pompeii from a book written by his mother.[1]

Linda Fierz-David was an unusual woman from the start. Born in Basel in 1891, she was the first woman in that city to be allowed to go to the university. She studied German linguistics but was not there too long before she met and married a fellow student, Hans Fierz, who was at the end of his studies in chemistry.

Her father was a politician who really thought of himself as a poet, and her mother was the daughter of a Galician Jew from Cracow and a Croatian countess of great elegance who could also read tarot cards and palms. Linda used to say that she got the poetic side of her nature from her father and his family and her witchcraft from her mother.

Linda could sing beautifully and music was an important part of her background. She had a brother who was a composer and who, according to her son, was a 'very wicked gentleman who preferred to live on the money of my mother's (Linda's) husband, which was an excellent idea because he contributed quite a bit to the education of my brothers and me.'

In 1918, after the First World War, a flu epidemic spread over Europe killing thousands of people. Linda became ill with it and almost died. When she finally recovered, it was discovered that she had contracted tuberculosis. She had to leave her family of four young sons and husband and go to a sanitorium in the Swiss Alps. It was a terrible wrench for her and for her family. She had been a devoted mother who had every night sung traditional Swiss songs while she accompanied herself on the piano, and told her boys fairy-tales which she herself wrote and illustrated, putting them into little books.

She went into a sanitorium which was filled with people of many nationalities, many of whom were still being treated for lungs damaged by poison gas in the war. It sounds very much like the clinic in Thomas Mann's novel, *The Magic Mountain*, where the patients, thrown together by their disease and very often with only that in common, formed a society all their own. They spoke of everything happening in the world which was shut off to them, and it was here, ironically, that Linda had to come to learn of the man in her own home city of Zurich who was such a marvellous healer of souls: C.G. Jung. She wrote to him, then went to consult with him, telling him of her life and the fact that she could not seem to find a way out of her illness. (She had then been in the sanitorium for four years.) Jung told her to remove herself from the sanitorium, enter a hotel and heal herself. Years later, in the Houston interview films of 1957, shown on television and then released as a commercial film, Jung made a statement to the effect that half the number of tubercular cases are psychic, and result from the fact that people under the influence of a complex breathe less deeply. He said, 'Some people have very shallow breathing, don't ventilate the apices of their lungs anymore and get tuberculosis.'[2] He felt that Linda Fierz-David should resume her academic studies and begin to read books. She followed his advice and within one year was cured of her disease and able to return to her family.

Once home, she found herself in a complicated situation. Her husband had an Italian cousin who was a very witty, charming and cultivated man, and who was also very handsome. He gradually became something like a

second husband to her, according to her son, Heinrich.
This was a tortuous situation for her as she remained in
love with her husband who was even more witty, charming and handsome. The three of them became close and
the conflict within her became so strong that once more
she went to consult Jung.

The most immediate result was that the figure of Jung
over-shadowed that of the cousin, and he himself came to
be the inspirer and 'god-like animus'. The cousin faded
into the background. He did not leave her life altogether,
but he was no longer the 'second husband'.

In fact, Jung entered the life of the entire Fierz-David
family. One of Linda's sons, Heinrich, even became a
Jungian analyst himself. Jung and his wife dined *en famille*
with them several times and at a party at their house an
event took place which reflects one of Jung's most attractive qualities: his spontaneity.

Hans Fierz-David, Linda's husband, had just told Jung,
'You have just complained that you are so tired by your
patients that you have had enough of your practice for
the time being. Very well. Tomorrow morning I leave for
Egypt and Palestine and I am going first class, which
means there is one unused bed on the train and the
ship. Please join me instead of complaining about your
practice.' Jung replied that he could do no such thing. It
was impossible. The next morning, Jung was at the train
with all his suitcases packed. They left together for the
Middle East.

In Alexandria, they were accosted by a palmist as they
left the ship. He read the hand of Professor Fierz-David,
then he took Jung's hand. 'Oh. You are one of the few
really great men that I have met. I cannot say more.'

This trip was to have important results for Jung. After
their return from the voyage, during which they amply
sampled the ship's wine cellar, Fierz-David saw to it that
Jung became a professor at the Swiss Federal Polytechnic
Institute in Zurich. Here Jung once more resumed his
academic career.

In the meantime, Linda devoted herself to psychology
and with Jung's encouragement became a Jungian

analyst. She also contributed some very fine studies to the body of Jungian knowledge. Her first studies had been in modern literature, and she gave several lectures on the psychological interpretation of literature. Then Jung asked her to work at deciphering a sort of Renaissance sign or picture language used in one of the most famous books of the Renaissance, *The Dream of Poliphilo* which is composed entirely of pictures from very fine woodcuts. It is also one of the most elusive and expensive volumes in the antiquarian book trade today. Linda interpreted it psychologically as the human search for soul or anima, and gave several lectures on it at the Zurich Psychological Club. Step by step, she turned the lectures into a book which was published in 1938.[3]

Linda, or 'Sieglinde', as Jung had by now nicknamed her, did her next major work on the frescoes at the Villa of Mysteries at Pompeii, finishing it shortly before her death in 1964. This fine book is rationally very well put together, and inspiration keeps breaking through as though the material was deeply felt and experienced, as well as intellectually understood. Given her trials and experiences with the other men in her life who appeared as counterpoints in her relationship to her husband, it is little wonder that the Dionysian thrust of the frescoes spoke to her in a very personal way. This book was previously only available in Jungian Institutes throughout the world, but is now generally available.[4]

The book is revealing of the author's own personality and beliefs. In one place, we see her feelings about the equality of women: 'As Guglielmo Ferrero said in his book *The Women of the Caesars*, placing women on an equal basis with men, *which we so gladly claim as our own high moral aim*, was first reached by women in Rome.' This was not necessarily the 'high moralism' of the late 1950s and early 1960s, and we are still struggling with it in the 1990s. It was certainly an aim of Fierz-David's.

Nor Hall, in her wonderful book, *Those Women*,[5] speaks of Fierz-David's material as being 'periodically epiphanic' and goes on to write, 'Breakthroughs of emotion, subjectivity and fantasy make her "scientifically objective" text sparkle. These moments of breakthrough often come with an apology appended or implied.' Considering just how subjectively much of Jung's material was gained, it seems strange that Fierz-David would need to add any apology to her treatment of intellectual material. However, it was important to Jung to be thought 'scientific' so that he would have his work taken seriously. Colin Wilson, in his biography of Jung,[6] writes of Jung's excitement at reading the introductory comment in Krafft-Ebing's *Textbook of Psychiatry*: 'It is probably due to the peculiarity of the subject and its incomplete state of development that psychiatric textbooks are stamped with a more-or-less subjective character.' He goes on: 'First of all the admission that psychiatry is *subjective* because it is undeveloped – an indication that it would have room for the subjective approach of a romantic idealist, and that therefore he could take his place among its pioneers.' So actually we see that Linda Fierz-David was simply 'following in the steps of the Master' when she lapsed into subjective stances. Given what she was attempting in approaching the frescoes, a subjective stance would have been almost a requirement. Nor Hall goes on to tell us that at one point Fierz-David claims to give 'rein a little to her fancy' about the uses of a tunnel. She goes on: 'breaking boundaries, whether it be of syntax, content or style, is a peculiarly Dionysian vehicle for the conveyance of new material'.

In his introduction to Fierz-David's work *The Dream of Poliphilo*, Jung speaks of her as being his Ariadne, which of course puts him in the role of Dionysus, another mythological theme running through his own personal psychology and the reason perhaps why he was forgiven some of his excesses of temper and indulgence.

In 1963, Fierz-David contracted stomach cancer. A few months before her death, she called the best dressmaker in Zurich, who had dressed her very elegantly all her life, and had him make her a dress which would disguise the distortions of her figure brought on by her illness. She then called a family meeting with her sons. As they arrived, she greeted them from her favourite chair, dressed in the new outfit that had been designed for the occasion. She offered her sons some sherry and snacks, and lit a cigarette for herself to give the appearance of normality. She then proceeded to tell them the contents of her will, including her plans regarding family properties. They told her they did not at all agree with her plan to give their property which bordered on Jung's Bollingen estate (which he had originally purchased from the Fierz-Davids) to Marie-Louise von Franz and Barbara Hannah. A compromise was reached whereby the two women received the right, as long as they lived, to visit when none of the sons was in residence. On this property Linda had built a pavilion, her own Villa of Mysteries. On the walls she painted 'mystic things, a secret language, a secret script'. Her son remembers that, from time to time, 'she burned a candle in this pavilion'.[7]

Toward the end she had to be hospitalised, but for the last two weeks of her life her son, Heinrich Fierz-Monnier, came to Zurich and brought her home and remained there with her until she died. He felt that Jung's understanding of the special relationship between mother and son enabled him to be closer to his mother in those last days.

Linda Fierz-David had had a little dog to whom she had been much attached as a middle-aged woman. The night this little dog died, she had a dream that a little old man went into the forest and did not return. The night that Linda died, her daughter-in-law had a dream that a little old lady went into the forest and did not return.

She died just three years after the death of the man whom she felt had given her back her life over forty years earlier.

Notes

The majority of the information on Linda Fierz-David in this chapter comes from an interview by the author with the son of Linda Fierz-David, the late Dr Heinrich Fierz-Monnier, which took place in the spring of 1978. Dr Fierz was a prominent Jungian analyst and for many years the Director of the Clinic and Research Centre for Jungian Psychology in Zurich. In his own right he was a fine analyst and unusual man with many gifts. Each year he would 'go into the forest', as he put it, to think of the right gift to give people when he would metamorphose into Sinterklaas (Santa Claus) for the annual Christmas party given for therapists and patients alike at the Clinic. I was fortunate enough to have therapy with him for the period I attended the Institute in Zurich. Not only did the therapy help me in a personal sense, but it was also liberally laced with stories of Jung and Dr Fierz's mother, Mrs Fierz-David. I am much indebted to Dr Fierz for his great kindness to me and the help and understanding he gave me when I was writing this book.

1. L. Fierz-David, *Women's Dionysian Initiation*.
2. McGuire and Hull (eds), *C.G. Jung Speaking*.
3. L. Fierz-David, *The Dream of Poliphilo*.
4. L. Fierz-David, *Women's Dionysian Initiation*.
5. N. Hall, *Those Women*.
6. C. Wilson, *Lord of the Underworld: Jung and the Twentieth Century*.
7. N. Hall, *Those Women*.

CHAPTER SEVEN

M. Esther Harding and the Mysteries of Woman

Of all the Jungian women, it is perhaps Dr Harding whose name is best known outside Jungian circles. Her book, *Woman's Mysteries*, must be one of the seminal books of the spiritual women's movement. It is invariably cited in feminist literature along with another of her books, *The Way of all Women*.

Her life had its start in the almost picture-postcard prettiness of the English countryside in Shropshire. The slow-paced, idyllic atmosphere of this part of Great Britain seems little preparation for the almost superhuman struggles she had to endure as that oddity at the turn of the century, the *lady* doctor. Yet she was to say to a friend at the end of her life, 'If you don't understand that I am Shropshire through and through, you don't understand me at all.'[1] Possibly it was that Shropshire strain that stood her in good stead throughout a gruelling internship at the Royal Infirmary in London, the only place that accepted women interns. After working for almost inhumanly long hours there, she and her friends would spend more hours listening to the Spanish guitar music which enthralled her at the time. Later, when she heard that Stravinsky's *Rite of Spring* was to have its premiere in London, she saved for months to have a seat at the performance instead of her more usual standing room. She said later, 'I knew that I was listening to a statement from the New World. High in the gallery that night I knew that the Victorian age was over.'[2] For the few women like herself, striving to make a place for themselves

44

in a world that was almost totally male, this must have been very good news indeed.

It was perhaps her rigorous training, and the scarcely believable insults that women in the medical profession had to bear, that made for the stiff discipline that she expected of herself and others to the end of her life. She was a hard taskmistress and not universally loved, to say the least.

She had been a doctor for six years when she attended Jung's first seminar in England, held in Sennen Cove, Cornwall. Sennen Cove was a place steeped in mystery: it was reputed to be frequented by mermaids, and a sort of 'living mist', known as the 'hooper' for the noise it made, hovered around the rocks. The locals regarded it as a protective spirit for the many fishermen of the neighbourhood. It was a particularly fitting place for a 'fisher of souls' like Jung, who was to find three of his strongest female disciples here. The seminar had as its topic the dreams from a book entitled *Peter Blobb's Dreams*. After the conference, Dr Harding followed Jung to Zurich as did Dr Constance Long and Dr Eleanor Bertine.

After working with Jung in Zurich for three years, Harding came to the United States and joined Dr Bertine, apparently at the suggestion of Dr Jung. She and Bertine became very close and lived together for the rest of their lives. Jung often did a spot of 'matchmaking' in this way. He felt that unmarried professional women in careers where they were virtually the only women would need the support of another woman in the same situation. He also sometimes did the same with women who were homosexual.

Once in the United States, Harding, Bertine and Kristine Mann joined forces and inaugurated the first Analytical Psychology Club in New York in 1936, and were later instrumental in founding the Institute in New York.

The latter was beset for a long time by an unusual problem. It seems that it was 'split down the middle' by two warring factions: those who were being analysed by homosexual analysts and those who were seeing

non-homosexual analysts. In the early days of the Institute, all the analysands knew one another as they all
attended the various lectures and events, much as in
Zurich. The sexual differences of the analysts caused a
great deal of ill-feeling. Many of the women (and men)
who were being analysed by the homosexuals wondered
whether their analysts could really help them with problems concerning heterosexual relationships. Those having
non-homosexual analysts generally believed they could
not. It made for some very heated discussions and led to
a great deal of tension. People who were there at the time
said they could literally 'see' the split. In the auditorium
where the lectures were presented, there were certain rows
that were used by one faction and off limits to the other.
This state of affairs lasted for many years until several of
the women had died.

Another source of tension was the presence at the
lectures of Dr Harding. She had a special seat in the
auditorium, quite close to the podium where the lecturer
stood, and the audience would watch her to see whether
she was nodding or shaking her head. Occasionally, she
would stand up abruptly and challenge the speaker in a
loud voice. Speakers who got wind of this habit would
look at her themselves from time to time to see how she
was taking it. If she did not get up during the lecture
itself she would sometimes do so afterwards, and 'dress
down' the speaker from the podium if she disagreed. Some
of the people in the audience close to her would, if she
were shaking her head, direct hostile questions to the
speaker afterward. One New York analyst, in order to
avoid those problems, said as little as possible in his first
lecture. As can be imagined, this state of affairs did not
lead to a relaxed atmosphere nor one conducive to the
development of thought.

Harding ruled the Institute with an iron fist not noticeably in a velvet glove. Anyone who wanted to get involved
had to first have a few hours with her. She is seldom
spoken of with much affection except by those who first
met her in later years when she had mellowed a little. Dr
Henderson has said that she made a distinct effort to

bring her feeling function to the fore at that time. Jung believed that thinking types often lack the conscious ability to feel and are prone to say things which hurt the feelings of others.

One of the women who worked with her, Margaret Barker, has written a moving portrait of her in later years. ' . . . like a wise old bird with that high clear note in her voice, ruffled at times . . . seemingly lacking in humour, a "thinking type", not a "feeling type" . . . suddenly there would come a moment of acute observation and the audience would laugh and Dr Harding would share in the laughter, fully like a young girl. The wise old bird had become approachable, the eagle more a gliding and settling gull, but sharp-eyed as ever.'[3]

Throughout the period of her involvement with analytical psychology, she, Bertine and Mann would take three month terms away every year, in rotation, to return to Zurich, to the font, and be analysed by Jung. Clearly they were among those who needed the renewing lifeline to the great man.

During one of the visits, Harding told Jung of a dream she had once had of a priest. He told her she had an animus like an archimandrite (the superior of a large monastery of the Orthodox Church). 'It is as if to say you are a priest of the mysteries. This takes a great humility to balance it. You need to go down to the level of mice.'[4] This humility was one of the things for which she strived.

The work that will insure her immortality, *Woman's Mysteries*, had its beginnings in her early days with Jung. She attended the English seminars which Jung regularly gave in Zurich. In one particular seminar they were studying the dreams of a man, in one of which there was a cauldron in which crescents and crosses were mixed. Half the seminar members were asked to study the symbolism of the cross and half that of the crescent. Harding's research was so vast and so interesting that Jung encouraged her to enlarge it and write it up for publication. This was the beginning of *Woman's Mysteries*. However, whether due to a remark of Jung's as some have

47

suggested, or to a decision of the publisher, it was many years before it was published.

Dr Henderson's remarks on an early draft are interesting in this context. 'One of the strands of (Harding's) research had to do with an intoxicating drink known as *soma*. Jung said, "First take some of the *soma* out of it." It is as if Esther and the fate of her research obeyed this injunction by withholding publication until *The Way of all Women* was published. In this work the intoxification of the archetypal imagery has been pushed into the background and the human message alone, maintaining the right balance between theory and practice shines forth.'[5]

I was first introduced to this book while it was still out of print and before it was taken up almost as a cult book by the spiritual women's movement, and for me it was nothing short of a revelation on the psychic roots of woman. Having only been exposed to Christianity and Judaism, it was stunning to learn that women had once held an honoured place in religion and that a female deity, in multiple forms, had been worshipped. It was no coincidence that it was put into my hands by a poet. Jung was fond of saying that perhaps only poets could really understand him and the same might be said of this work of Harding's. At the time it was published, it was as shocking and as mind-boggling in its implications as *The White Goddess* by Robert Graves, possibly more so as the material is presented in a low-key, understandable way accessible to a greater readership. For many women it restored the link between their ancestresses and their own inner experiences. Equally Jung, whose attitude was still influenced by the patriarchal attitudes of his generation, was shocked by it. As we shall see in the later part of this book, Jung still had a fear and distaste for the aggressive feminine and the mixture in *Woman's Mysteries* might have been too much for him until he digested it. I never found its tone ecstatic, but reading it sometimes felt ecstatic. It is a remarkable piece of research and it is hard to believe that it was conceived as early as 1929. What might have happened had it been published then, it is impossible to say. Perhaps Jung sensed it was ahead of its time. And perhaps its knowledge of the inner realms of woman was a revelation to him also: he admitted several times that only women could know what was within Woman.

I could choose many passages to quote, and the following may not be revolutionary now but were certainly so when they were first written. 'For to women, life itself is cyclic. The life force ebbs and flows in her actual experience, not only in nightly and daily rhythm as it does for a man but also in moon cycles . . . ' 'The feminine essence, when it is talked about, is no longer the true feminine essence; or as Dr Jung once expressed it in poetical terms, "Yin is like a mother-of-pearl image hidden in the deepest recesses of the house."' And most revolutionary of all, 'Perhaps if more attention were directed to reinstating the goddess in the individual life, through psychological experiences, the modern equivalent to the initiations of the moon goddess, a way out . . . might open before us.' The following passage may even be a kind of self description: ' . . . a woman who is virgin, one-in-herself, does what she does – not because of any desire to please, not to be liked, or to be approved, even by herself; not because of any desire to gain power over another, to gain his interest or love, but because what she does is true.'[6]

Between them Bertine, Mann and Harding spread the Jungian word all over the eastern United States. Harding went on to write several more books on Jungian topics; her literary output was perhaps only equalled by that of von Franz. Along with Bertine and Mann, she was also instrumental in setting up the first Bailey Island conference in 1937 at which Jung gave an American seminar.

Although her yearly visits to Jung were the wellspring from which she drew her spiritual and mental energy, the house she shared with Bertine and Mann on Bailey Island, which was named Inner Ledges, was also a source of renewal. There she kept a garden, and among the plants she had a ground cover native to her home in Shropshire, which she encouraged to grow in Maine. Like herself, it seemed to thrive in its adopted land.

In the last years of her life she took to wearing a black felt hat, regarded by those who saw her in it with astonishment and horror. In this monstrosity, combined with outsize black glasses to protect her eyes, she set out for what was to be her last journey. One of her friends took her to the airport, feeling that her whole ensemble gave her a 'forbidding, Fellini-like look.'[7] The trip was her first to Greece, the home of the women's mysteries of which she had written. She also got to see Jung's tower at Bollingen, which for one reason or another she had never managed to see on her visits to Jung. Her last stop was the family home in Shropshire which she had not visited in ten years. A few days later, in the airport hotel, she died in her sleep. She was eighty-three years old.

She left a fortune of one million dollars to the New York Institute when she died. She may well be judged, by generations of women, to have made the most outstanding contribution to the literature of women's psychology.

Notes

1. W. Kennedy, 'Esther Harding: To Greece and Home', *Quadrant Magazine*, Autumn 1971 (Memorial issue to Esther Harding).
2. S. van Culin, 'Esther Harding and Stravinsky', *Quadrant Magazine*, Autumn 1971.
3. M. Barker, 'Images of Transformation', *Quadrant Magazine*, Autumn 1971.
4. 'Esther Harding's Notebooks', *Quadrant Magazine*, Spring 1975.
5. Esther Harding obituary by Dr Joseph Henderson, San Francisco Institute.
6. M. Esther Harding, *Woman's Mysteries*.
7. W. Kennedy, 'Esther Harding: To Greece and Home', *Quadrant Magazine*, Autumn 1971.

CHAPTER EIGHT

Kristine Mann and Eleanor Bertine

The lives of Kristine Mann and Eleanor Bertine are linked in so many places that it seems fitting that they should share a chapter. Mann was fourteen years Bertine's senior and both were born in the eastern United States; Mann in New Jersey and Bertine in New York. Mann's parents were Swedenborgians, a mystical Christian sect founded in the nineteenth century by Emmanuel Swedenborg, a very good background for an understanding of Jungian psychology. She remained a Swedenborgian all her life.

Mann graduated from Smith College in 1899 and proceeded to teach science, history and English at various schools, including Briarly School of New York and Vassar. She then decided on a medical career and graduated from Cornell in 1913.

In the meantime, one of the young women whom she had taught at Vassar, Eleanor Bertine, graduated *summa cum laude* and Phi Beta Kappa from that college. She announced to her parents that she intended to go to medical school. They begged her to reconsider: medicine was not a fit career for a woman. She thought it over for a year at their request, then went on to Cornell Medical School where she was one of only three women in her class. Mann was one of the other two.

Mann's chief interest was health education for women and on graduation from medical school she worked in that area. Meanwhile, Bertine did an internship at Bellevue Hospital in New York and seemed to have been interested in psychiatry from the beginning. She was also a consulting physician at the New York Reformatory for Women

51

where she found conditions so terrible that she resigned in protest.

After the First World War Bertine played a key role in putting together a programme for an international conference for women physicians for the War Work Council of the Young Women's Christian Association. Women doctors came from over fifteen countries to hear lectures on such subjects as 'health and morality in the light of the new psychology'. Her views were very advanced for the time, as such remarks as the following indicate: 'I can conceive of circumstances under which a so-called immoral act might be a real step toward the development of an individual'. Very heady stuff for a society which was only just beginning to lift the hems of the skirts to a workable length.

Both she and Mann seem to have been influenced at this time by another woman doctor practising at the Cornell Medical School: Dr Beatrice Hinkle. Dr Hinkle had moved east from San Francisco where she had been the first woman to hold a public health position as City Physician. Upon her arrival in New York, she opened the first psychotherapeutic clinic in America at Cornell Medical School. Shortly thereafter she went to Europe to investigate the work of C.G. Jung, who was then a new name in psychiatry. She can be seen in the photograph of the Weimar Conference, standing near Emma and Jung. She is particularly noticeable because of her good looks.

Hinkle was so impressed with Jung that she undertook the first English translation of his *Psychology of the Unconscious*, and subsequently found a publisher. She thereby launched Jung's American reputation and was instrumental in making him available to many English-speaking people who otherwise would not have had access to his work. As time went on, her translation was found to be not as precise as Jung wished and that by C.F. Baynes, the wife of Peter Godwin Baynes, both of whom did a great deal of translating of Jung's work, supplanted it. Hinkle also undertook to write a book with a similar typology to Jung's but differing on many critical points. Though she remained an analyst and friend of the three

New York women, she was never really thought of as a Jungian again.

In 1920, Eleanor Bertine went to England for analysis along with Dr Constance Long. Dr Long was one of those responsible for bringing Jung to speak at his first seminar in England, at Sennen Cove. It was attended by only twelve people, a size Jung felt most congenial. It was there that Bertine first met Jung, as well as Dr Esther Harding. Bertine was so impressed by Jung that she followed him back to Zurich, as did Harding, where she remained for a couple of years, studying and undergoing analysis. She wrote to her friend, Kristine Mann, who then went to Zurich herself in 1921, also to study with Jung.

In 1922, Drs Hinkle, Mann and Bertine, who remained lifelong friends, returned to the United States to pioneer Jungian analysis on the east coast. Dr Constance Long was with them, but died an untimely death shortly after her arrival. Dr Harding joined them in 1923. Bertine and Harding took an apartment together and gave small dinner parties, invitations to which were highly prized. Together with Mann they founded the New York Analytical Psychology Club in 1936 and also planned for Jung's Bailey Island Seminar in 1937. One hundred people showed up which rather overwhelmed Jung, who much preferred small gatherings. After it was over, he and Emma arrived in England quite exhausted by all the people and activity.

All three women led long, productive and creative lives, supporting one another and remaining close to Jung. Dr Mann was the first to die in 1945 at the age of sixty-three. Dr Bertine died in 1968 aged eighty-one years old, still an analyst and still active in the Club. Dr Harding lived the longest, dying in 1971, her eighty-third year after fulfilling (as we have seen) her lifelong ambition of going to Eleusis in Greece where the Great Goddess had reigned supreme.

The part played by these women in widening the influence of Jung's psychology cannot be overestimated. Jung valued them and their work and kept in regular contact with them until his own death in 1961. That they were forbidding and difficult is certainly true, but given their contributions, much can be forgiven.

CHAPTER NINE

Jolande Jacobi: Impressario

'Sol Hurok presents ... Jung!' This was the answer I received when I asked why Jolande Jacobi, herself a Jungian analyst, incurred the wrath of so many of her fellow-analysts.[1] Jacobi was the disturber of the peace, the one with the vision of Jung's greatness who wished to present him to the world in a big way; an extrovert who grated on the nerves of the very introverted circle of people around Jung. One can also detect a note of envy with this criticism, however, because she was the one who knew how to deal with the public, and this helped Jung survive as time went on and his fame grew. She learned the tools for survival very early in her own life.

Jolande Szejacs was born into a world of privilege in Budapest in 1890. Her father was a senator and wealthy manufacturer. Both parents were of Jewish background but were baptised Catholics. She married another wealthy man when she was only nineteen, a prominent attorney, Dr Andreas Jacobi. She had two sons by him, but was restless at home and took a secretarial course so that she might help her husband in his office. While studying, she made friends with someone who helped her escape with her husband and children to Vienna after a communist takeover in Budapest in 1919. The family remained there after the fall of the communist government: Vienna was a city that allowed more scope for her prodigious energies. In 1925, her husband returned to Budapest but left his family in Vienna where he wished his sons to be educated. He thereafter divided his time between the two cities.

In 1926, Jacobi became involved with the Austrian Kulturbund in Vienna and soon became its vice-president, arranging lectures from famous names in the arts throughout

55

Europe until 1938. She had kept her visitor's book from her stay in Vienna and it reads like a cultural history of the time: Béla Bartók, Paul Valery, Heinrich Zimmer, and . . . C.G. Jung.

She had met Jung in 1927 when he came to lecture at the Kulturbund, and gave a luncheon in her apartment for the great man and his admirers. Jung stayed behind after all the visitors had left, and told her about the I Ching. She was very impressed that he could write out all sixty-four hexagrams from memory.

Later on in that year, she had a dream which she describes in one of her books, though anonymously: '. . . the dream of a thirty-eight year old woman who is married. She dreamt it for the first time shortly after meeting Jung – socially, not professionally. She had no notion of psychology, let alone of Jung's depth psychology, and no knowledge of even the most elementary psychological concepts, nor had she ever dealt with dreams, so that the dream, which shook her to the depths, found her quite unprepared, unarmed by any foreknowledge, and yet seemed to point the way.

'The action of the dream took place at first in the bay of a beautiful baroque castle, in a high room with twelve corners, the walls and ceiling of which were covered with mirrors. The room was completely empty. The dreamer was lying fully dressed on the smooth parquet floor, which like a *troittoir roulant*, revolved around a finely chased metal knob to which she held fast with her hands. Seeing herself reflected on all sides as well as from above, threw herself into the greatest confusion: distorted, chopped to pieces, she could hardly recognise herself. To begin with the floor moved quite slowly, then it got faster and faster until it spun around like mad and made her completely dizzy. Her clothes fell away from her and she was seized with a terrible fear that she might not be able to hold on to the knob and would be flung by centrifugal force of the movement into the wall mirrors, where she might be fatally wounded. In vain she tried to hang on. Helpless, naked and terrified she finally crashed against the wall, which shattered into a thousand pieces and seemed to engulf her. Then the room and castle vanished.

'Still alive, but bleeding from a thousand wounds, the dreamer now lay out of doors, naked on her back in a freshly ploughed field. All round was silence. A pallid February sun lit the scene nearing the zenith. On her left sat a man, the man she loved dressed in a long white shirt, weeping. His tears wetted the shirt. With the wet patches he gently wiped the dreamer's wounds until they closed up, healed. Thankfully she looked up at him and the sky. Suddenly she felt the earth beginning to move beneath her, as though it were growing together with her back. At the same time she felt the man was no longer by her side, but was stretched out on top of her motionless and weighing a ton. The weight pressed on her deeper and deeper down, but the earth seemed to go on thrusting and pushed her upwards. As it continued to push, the piled-up mounds of earth began to sprout. Grass shot up in the air, the field became a verdant meadow, and the dreamer became one with it. She herself was the earth, the blossoming nature. But the man who lay on top of her grew lighter and lighter as she grew together with the earth. Soon he seemed to have melted into air; he became the firmament arching above the meadow. Thus they cele-brated the marriage of heaven and earth, the union of the masculine and feminine principle.'[2]

She sent the dream to Jung in Zurich and he replied that she was now 'caught' and could not get away.

The next couple of years were indeed a turning point in her life. The man with whom she had been very close became ill and died very slowly over a three-year period. His receiving of the rite of extreme unction while on the point of death shook Jacobi. She claimed that it was at this time that she decided to become a practising Catholic.

Jacobi wrote to Jung to ask if he would train her as an analyst, to which he replied he would only if she first received a doctorate. One version of this story has it that he said this, hoping to discourage her, never dreaming she should attempt such a thing at forty-four years old. If true, he reckoned without her tremendous energy. She enrolled at the University of Vienna and began her study of psychology. At this time, however, Hitler's shadow was already beginning to spread over the world. In 1938, four months before she was due to get her degree, the Nazis marched in Austria. Since she was so prominent in the Kulturbund, she came under the scrutiny of the invaders and returned one day to find that her apartment had been ransacked by the Gestapo. She returned posthaste to Budapest.

From Budapest she told Jung what had happened and asked that she might come there right away. He replied that he was sorry, but she had to have her degree first. This seems rather bizarre, particularly in view of the fact that many of the women in his circle who were practising analysts never had *any* degree. If he was trying once more to discourage her, he had picked a rather dangerous, sadistic way to do it. In any case, she could not be stopped. Once again she proved her courage and returned to Vienna, fearing for her life but determined to get her degree and go to Zurich. She stayed at the apartment of a friend, and pretending to be in mourning, went about heavily veiled and won her degree. In October 1938 she came to Zurich, degree in hand. She was then forty-nine years old.

One of her sons was able to get out of Hungary and join her in Switzerland, but the other had to wait until the war was over. The rest of her family she lost to the Nazis when they entered Hungary. Her mother and father committed suicide when faced with deportation and her husband died on his way to the internment camp. It was a story like so many others at the time.

Once more she had to begin life all over again. From the beginning, she had problems with other Jungian analysts, mostly the women, some of which was due to the fact that she very often voiced what she was thinking without first pausing to reflect. Barbara Hannah was heard to say that 'Jolande always had her front feet in the trough.' In a letter to Jacobi, dated 1941, after she had been in Zurich three years, Jung cautioned her, 'Watch your tongue; it can sting . . . '3

Her relationship with Jung was always chancy, as the latter was also inclined to sharp words. Together they made for a very explosive combination as the following anecdote from a San Francisco analyst shows. This analyst had been coming to Jung for analysis at 8 a.m. Jung had so many demands on his time that he began work even earlier, with an appointment with Jacobi at 7 a.m. The stairs leading up to the room where he saw patients were divided by a landing half way, then led off to the right, to his door. One morning, '. . . as I started up the stairs, I heard the door above bang open as if it had been charged by a buffalo and I heard Jung yelling "raus, raus, raus." [out, out, out!] and the next thing I heard as I walked up the stairs, electrified by this bellow, was the unmistakeable sound of a woman's bottom going "bump, bump, bump" down the stairs. I arrived at the middle landing at the same time that she [Dr Jacobi] arrived on her bottom from the top of the stairs. Her skirts were up over her head. She got up (she was not easily shy or embarrassed) and pulled her skirts down to where they were supposed to be . . . and she bowed me and said, "Gruezi, Herr Doktor" and I said, "Gruezi Frau Doktor" and she walked down the stairs, this time on her feet. (Upstairs when I arrived) Jung was pouring quarts of spit (out of his pipe stem which he did when annoyed). When he wasn't doing this he was running up and down the office. I said, "Is it indiscreet of me to . . . ?" He said, "No! It is not indiscreet! She came here saying she wanted to write a book. But that's not it. She wants to pick my brains and she wants analysis with me !" '[4]

A few years later, at an Analytical Psychology Club meeting in San Francisco, I heard confirmation of this story when an older woman was remembering how Jung showed her the staircase and said, 'You see that staircase? I threw Jolande Jacobi down that once. She is such an impossible woman!'

Despite all this, in her forty years as an analyst and prime mover in analytical psychology, Dr Jolande Jacobi wrote several good books on Jung's psychology. Occasionally one of her own ideas will creep through as in this passage in *The Psychology of C.G. Jung* which refers to the predominance of feeling types in women; 'They seem to make up a fairly high percentage of their sex, though there may have been some change since the turn of the century, perhaps as a result of the emancipation of woman'.[5] For the most part, however, the books stick closely to Jung's words and ideas, simply clarifying him. Possibly Jung, who knew only too well how difficult his writing was for many people, was fearful of the popularisation of his ideas and, in his introverted way, distrusted her simplification and clarity. He needn't have worried, for despite the clarity of Jacobi's books, many of the precepts of Jungian psychology still escape the ordinary lay reader.

In an obituary on Jacobi, Baroness Vera von der Heydt wrote that 'When she presented him with *Psychological Reflections*, which is an anthology of Jung's ideas, as a gift for him on his seventieth birthday, his only comment was, "So you want people to read what you have put together instead of reading my books?" Jolande had obviously minded about the incident, but she was tough and was used to attacks and hostility and was smiling when she told me this story.'[6]

Jung may have been jealous of, and irritated by, Jacobi, yet she was a good efficient extrovert and a marvellous salesperson. She was also a charming hostess and quite attractive to men. Jung knew that he could not have done much of the work she did for the Institute and for his psychology. She was aggressive (pushy and brassy according to her detractors), but these are not negative qualities when dealing with the outside world. The rest of the women were all introverts and could never have brought themselves to do what she did.

In later years when I met her at the Institute a few months before her death, she did the Institute (and me) a great service. I was in charge for a time of arranging receptions for guest speakers. I was appalled when practically no students showed up for a party given for a very distinguished guest who had given a rather boring lecture earlier that day. Then I thought of Dr Jacobi and I sent a car for her with a message explaining our predicament. Scarcely half an hour later, she arrived in a brocaded dress, modest jewels and a perfumed fur wrap. She immediately took over with the guest of honour, smoothed his ruffled feathers, and charmed him thoroughly. I am certain that he never gave a second thought to how few people were present, after she arrived. She was then eighty-two years old. I wished that night that I had had the privilege of knowing her forty years earlier.

It was she who drew up the original plan for the Institute. It is said that it was so comprehensive that it was akin to the charter for the United Nations. It had everything in it, but was easily scaled down to size. She wanted to do everything in a big way, as always; it was perhaps her impressario nature. Or maybe the grand scale of Vienna between the wars was overpowering in the smaller, more provincial atmosphere of Zurich.

When Jung finally consented to have an Institute in his name (although he said it made him feel somehow less personal), Jolande Jacobi was one of the people whom he put on the Curatorium or Board of Governors. She did a great deal of good, for she was the one person who knew how to put on a great front for the world on its own terms. In the early days she greeted new arrivals, and she knew how to talk to them, and how to present the Institute in such a way as to make people feel they were really there instead of just drifting around in their own personal analyses.

If Jacobi could relate to the world, she had more of a problem with the other women in the circle. Matters were not helped, as we have seen, by her sharp tongue, but there is also the fact that they were jealous of her, and perhaps her indifferent behaviour toward other women angered them. Surprisingly, one of the only women with whom she did not have a problem was Toni Wolff, who seemed to command her respect, perhaps because Toni was a male-directed woman too. When Toni died, Yolande told Dr Henderson, 'She was like a rock. She could not be moved.'[7]

She had a good sense of humour and was able to laugh

at herself, which took the sharp edge off her frankness. However, she often put other women's backs up by her rather high-handed attitude, which might have been prompted by her own jealousies and the feeling of being an outsider to the charmed circle.

One woman told me that she had been invited to a party at Dr Jacobi's house just before the war. It was more like a Viennese salon with its marble statues and floor to ceiling paintings of classical subjects, and was quite grand by more reserved Swiss standards. At this party, my informant told me that she made the acquaintance of a young man her own age and they were deeply involved in their own conversation. Dr Jacobi came over and almost lifted the young woman off her feet, saying, 'You have monopolised enough of his time', and promptly took her place with him. The younger woman, being American and more outspoken, told her to 'go to hell', but Dr Jacobi remained where she was, apparently unruffled.

As an analyst, we have one modern account from a present-day Jungian therapist and writer, Robert Johnson: 'I began analysis with Yolande (sic) Jacobi, who is probably the most unfortunate choice I could have made – I being the introverted feeling type that I am, and she being an extroverted Hungarian, who conducted her analytical hours pacing the floor, which always annoyed me. She told me that the apartment owner, next floor down, took her to court in Switzerland because she paced. The Swiss judge heard her plea that "I am Hungarian and I pace, that is part of my nature, it is my right to pace", and he said, "All right, you may pace between 8 a.m. and 10 p.m., but not in the night"'.[8]

She was an original, and like many such, full of contradictions. She was the 'locomotive' and the 'ice-breaker'; some of her other nicknames are unfit to print. She was also one of the clearest expositors of Jung's thought, and Austria valued her services at the Kulturbund so highly, that in addition to the Knight's Cross of the Austrian Order of Service which she had been awarded in the 1930s, she was given honorary citizenship in 1957, something she prized very highly.

Her interview with me, when she said she was hard of hearing and couldn't seem to understand why I had come to Zurich, was very revealing. I had explained that I was recently divorced and just out of a serious illness and had come to the Institute to find some meaning to it all. She apparently didn't understand what I meant because she said, 'Oh, if you study too much, you will never get married again. Men *hate* smart women. Of course you might marry a man from one of the emerging African nations. They seem to appreciate intelligence'. Despite my protests that I was not interested in remarrying, she kept up this train of thought and came to the conclusion that it wasn't wise for a woman to be too smart. I felt she was speaking more from her own life experience than from mine.

She died in 1973, just short of eighty-three years old, and there have been no extroverted Jungian women who have since taken her place.

Notes

1. Dr Joseph Henderson, author's interview, November 1977.
2. J. Jacobi, *The Way of Individuation.*
3. G. Adler (ed.), *C.G. Jung Letters,* Vol. I 1906–1950.
4. Dr Joseph Wheelwright, author's interview, 1977.
5. J. Jacobi, *The Psychology of C.G. Jung.*
6. V. von der Heydt, Obituary of Jolande Jacobi, *Quadrant Magazine,* 1973.
7. Jane Wheelwright, author's interview, 1977.
8. M. Berger and S. Segaller, *Wisdom of the Dream.* Interview with Robert Johnson.

Much of the material in this chapter comes from an interview and subsequent brief acquaintance with Dr Jacobi in the autumn of 1972.

CHAPTER TEN

Marie-Louise von Franz: the Alchemist's Daughter

' "You know, Dr Jung, I think that 'Malus' is the best of the bunch." Jung said, "Yes, she is." '[1]

Born in 1915, she is the youngest of the women around Jung, the last to come to him and also the one who has made the biggest impact on the other Jungians: Marie-Louise von Franz. She is known affectionately by the Swiss diminutive 'Malus'. The Munich-born daughter of an Austrian nobleman, she is known chiefly for her formidable writings on such subjects as alchemy and numerology, and the interpretation of fairy-tales. She is also important for the authority of her views on what Jung would or would not have approved of on matters relating to the Institute and to other Jungian domains. A few years back, she split the Zurich Institute down the middle when she walked out after it was decided to offer a class on the dynamics of group therapy. She was firmly convinced that Jung, who had come out against the group process, would never have approved of it. What she does not appear to have taken into consideration is that this incident occurred twelve years after his death and that Jung changed his mind over and over again as he gathered more evidence on a variety of subjects.

She seems often to be one of those who fossilise theories by their adherence to them. She refused to appear or teach at the Institute and those very close to her refused also. A year later, the Institute capitulated, mainly because she was one of its shining lights. She came back and the anathema of group therapy was not mentioned again.

Marie-Louise is perhaps the most introverted of any of the women and has consistently refused to be interviewed or have publicity of any kind, though in her last years she is softening somewhat, having made brief appearances in two films about Jung; *Matter of Heart* and *The Wisdom of the Dream*. Most of her life has been lived quietly outside Zurich with Barbara Hannah, until Hannah's death a few years ago. According to Hannah's biography of Jung, it was his suggestion that they should live together.

In a BBC broadcast for the Jungian centenary celebrations, she gave a rare interview and spoke of their first meeting. 'Suddenly out of the bushes, what seemed an enormous man came with a dirty shirt and dirty trousers and gold-rimmed spectacles and I thought, "what an incredible face he has". He was very friendly. I felt terribly shy and he just shook our hands and said, "I haven't finished cooking. You boys go down and look at the lake and my sailing boat down there." And then he called me and said, "Could you cut these cucumbers up?" In great excitement I did and cut my thumb and the blood ran into the cucumber. And Jung just roared with laughter and gave me a bandage and so everything began.' In her verbal account von Franz takes on the tone of that eighteen-year-old girl.

Later on, after lunch, he began to talk to the students. 'For minutes I thought, "Now am I crazy or is this man crazy?" I can't see what he is driving at. Until I realised that for him the soul was real, and I became tremendously enthusiastic. We stayed until midnight and he poured a lot of wonderful burgundy down us and so I came home completely happy.'[2]

Marie-Louise graduated from the university with a doctorate in linguistics and immediately became an assistant of Jung's. Her life has been an offering dedicated to research and to the psychology of Jung.

It was von Franz whom Jung asked to finish the work started on the Grail by Emma Jung. Emma ostensibly started this work as a way of redeeming an ancestor who had failed in his quest of it. The book first came out in 1980 as *The Grail Legend* by Emma Jung and Marie-Louise von Franz.

It was also von Franz who became Jung's collaborator in the alchemical studies which were to be one of the major focuses of his later research. She translated one of the most valuable works in alchemy, *The Aurora Consurgens*. She was said to have been bitterly disappointed when it was not included in *The Collected Works*. If this story is true, then it would demonstrate conclusively just how closely she identifies her work with him. An excerpt from a work of hers, *The Feminine in Fairytales*, seems to underline her own relationship to her work: 'Many young girls refrain from studying or developing their minds, because *they rightly feel* [italics mine] that if they did they would fall into animus possession and that would prevent them from marrying.'[3] The idea that intellectual work precludes a happy marriage seems to come up time and again in the work of Jungian women, and certainly, as we have seen in this book, the majority of them did not marry, perhaps transferring the energy they would have expended on a relationship on to Jung. Later, in the same work, she speaks a bit poignantly of the loneliness of such a life and how a woman needs to accept it. 'According to my experience, it is very painful, but very important for women to realise and accept their loneliness.'[4]

Ambivalent feelings seem to flourish around von Franz as they did around all the Jungian women. Part of this is, as one Jungian said to me, 'the strain one feels being around her because she is so brainy'. The most common charge levelled against her is the 'freeze' she appears to put on the continued growth and development of Jung's ideas. As Jung is now dead, it is hard to understand why she would not wish to permit growth from his ideas as this is surely the way in which his psychology will remain the alive, viable philosophy it was during his lifetime. Jung himself, in this context, once stated that he was glad he was Jung and not a Jungian. Dr James Hillman, one of the most prominent, and perhaps the most brilliant, of the male analysts has gone so far as to drop the term

'Jungian' and refers to the psychology as 'archetypal'. So far this term is used only by Hillman and others like him. Several critics see the work of von Franz as building upon Jung's basic assumptions without necessarily validating them from experience or questioning the premises. When I mentioned this to one of the other women she said, 'And why not?' Therein may lie the problem.

Everyone agrees on one thing about von Franz: her brilliance. But it is a brilliance that can be maddeningly obscure at times, and that takes for granted that the reader has read all the same sources and is as erudite as she is. Her biography of Jung was long awaited, but when it appeared it was so laced with alchemical symbols and references from mythology and fairy-tales that many people, Jungians included, got lost in its obscurities, and put it down and picked it up over and over again, hoping to find its kernel.

Although she lived many years with Hannah, she was and continues to be very much of a loner. Perhaps her most pleasant times are spent at the tower she built for herself at Bollingen near Jung's Tower. She feels close to nature, in fact feels it is the natural domain of women: 'Women have a very deep relationship to Nature in its positive form'.[5]

She is very humble about her own intelligence and makes friends easily with non-intellectual people, as did Jung. She has said that she would like more women friends but that she is 'all thumbs with them'. This again seems a common theme with many of the women around Jung and although in analysis it is deemed necessary for women to make the connection to the feminine and therefore to other women, this does not seem to have occurred much with many of them. Her analyses with men appear to have run much smoother, and they found her easier to relate to than did many women.

Von Franz seems to have been closer to Jung than almost anyone outside his family in his last years and she appears to feel very much responsible for carrying on his work. She once told of a dream where a stack of Jung's writings on alchemy dropped to the ground and a tremendous wind came and started blowing all the papers away. She had to run around, collecting all the pages and putting them together again. The dream seems symbolic of the way she views herself and her relationship to Jung and his work. Perhaps it is why she clings so tenaciously to his written word and fears that new ideas such as the group class at the Institute will 'blow all the papers away'. In some way, though the winds of change may come and scatter his work, she is the one who must hold it all together and see that it remains of one piece. Quite a task for a small, frail woman now in her eighties, who is quite ill herself.

Her latest work is entitled *On Death and Dying* and because of her frail health, much of her attention is focused on this theme: 'It is only now, that I have dreamed it is finished, and I've done my work, that I see the pattern. In old age, one turns away from outer activity more, and one begins to reflect and to summarise whatever I have done up till now and what for and has it any meaning or is it meaningless, a certain fear of death which makes one prepare to be concerned with death . . . what is life, what is the meaning of life, why have I lived . . . was it worthwhile?'[6] And, ' . . . probably the reason for my illness. I've overworked all my life, my illness is an exhaustion illness.'[7]

After writing this chapter, I feel very frustrated because of the difficulty of speaking directly with von Franz. I wrote the following dream in my journal: 'I was with Marie-Louise von Franz. She had just completed a large, semi-sculptural collage which she was going to give to a patient. On it were two dinosaurs in bas-relief. In their loving arms they cradled the broken and battered body of a woman, still alive, whom von Franz was analysing.'

I was touched that von Franz could demonstrate so movingly that although the unconscious is filled with ancient monsters, they have a caring side. I thought to myself, 'Now I will have to show in the section on her that she has more feeling than I thought.'

Notes

1. Jane Wheelwright, author's interview, November 1977.
2. BBC Centenary Celebration of Jung's Life, 1975.
3. M.L. von Franz, *The Feminine in Fairy-Tales*.
4. Ibid.
5. Ibid.
6. S. Segaller and M. Berger, *The Wisdom of the Dream: The World of C.G. Jung*.
7. Ibid.

CHAPTER ELEVEN

Olga Frobe-Kapteyn and Eranos

'Don't go to Ascona; the föhn blows all the time and it is full of ladies with transferences!'[1] Dr F.M. Cornford of Oxford University took this advice from Heinrich Zimmer and was scared enough to turn down an invitation to speak at the Eranos Conference at Ascona.

For those who have not been to Switzerland, the föhn is a wind that blows off the Swiss Alps and is blamed by the Swiss for everything from nervous tension to sinus headaches. The 'ladies with transferences', of course, comprised the Valkyries and a variety of other women who were admirers of C.G. Jung. Ascona is the home of the Eranos Conferences which began in the early 1930s and which continue to this day, every summer, many years after the death of the dynamic woman whose vision they were.

Frau Frobe-Kapteyn's young husband died during the First World War, and soon after the war ended she came to live at the Casa Gabriella, the villa left to her by her father, along with a large parcel of adjoining land, on the shores of Lake Maggiore, near Ascona. Once there she went into virtual seclusion, studying the Vedanta and other Indian religious philosophies. She remained engrossed in these studies for seven years, seeing no other person but her servant until the outbreak of a neurosis which forced her to seek help in Zurich from Dr Jung.

After working with her for a while, Jung felt that such a secluded life had caused problems for the naturally extroverted woman. He suggested that she should share her interest in Oriental philosophy with others of similar

persuasion. She went back to Ascona and built a conference hall which was linked to her villa by a terraced
garden. This she had done intuitively, before it was really
clear to her just what it was she wished to do there.

Then she came up with the idea of a summer conference
in which scholars from different disciplines would each
present a paper. According to Barbara Hannah[2] her first
attempts were mixed in with metaphysics and it wasn't
until 1933 that she decided to bring her conference to a
truly scholarly level. According to another source, however, she came up with the idea of a scholarly conference
without any occult preliminaries.

In any case, the conference of 1933, the first recorded,
had the general theme of 'yoga and meditation in the East
and West'. She sent off letters of invitation to several
renowned professors of the day, and included among them
was the name of C.G. Jung. He flatly refused, saying she
wasn't going to 'pick his brain'. A rather strange reply
for the man who had been instrumental in setting her to
work on her own vision.

When she had her letters of acceptance from most of
the people she had contacted, she went to Jung and
showed him the list of speakers. After looking at it, he
said, 'You devil! You've invited all my friends and colleagues! Of course I'll come.'

Among the conference delegates was Dr Rudolf Otto,
author of *The Idea of the Holy*, and it was he who gave the
conference its name. 'Eranos' is a Greek word meaning a
feast to which everyone brings his own offering. Jung's
offering for this first conference was an empirical study of
the process of individuation. Toni Wolff made a copy of
the speech which can be found in the *Collected Works*. And
so the Eranos Tagung began, a yearly conference presented at Frau Kapteyn's Casa Maggiore.

Thus began for Jung a very fruitful yearly event at
which he was able to meet many people he might not
otherwise have done, and where he began many of his
closest associations with other scholars. It also gave him
another place to try out new material with which he was
working. Ira Progoff has written: 'I had observed that

each time Jung spoke at Eranos, it seemed to become the occasion for breaking new ground in his thinking. Certainly the thought occurred to me that perhaps the atmosphere of Eranos had something to do with it.'[3]

The atmosphere at Eranos was not, as might be expected, that of a scholarly ivory tower. For one thing, all the women around Jung flocked to it, not only to hear him speak but for a chance to really speak *to* him. In the normal course of events this was becoming more difficult as Jung's fame grew and more patients were coming to him. Even the Psychological Club lectures and appearances and those at the English Seminars had to be shared with too many others to be satisfactory. But as attendance at Eranos Conferences was limited because of the size of the surrounding towns for accommodation purposes, it provided a good opportunity to see Jung with only a few others, mostly of the inner circle, around him. Several people at the early conferences complained that they were hardly able to get near him because he was always surrounded by female admirers who came to be dubbed 'the Jungfrauen.'

One woman described the scene thus: ' . . . when the lecture was over, Jung used to sit on this wall, and in a flash we were clustering around him like bees around a honey pot, much to the annoyance of other participants . . . '[4] Note the image of the bees, which conjures up that of the priestess-bees of Aphrodite, surrounding the Son-God. But if he could be a stand-in for Aphrodite's son-lover, Jung could also summon up echoes of a more mischief-making god, Dionysus.

This form was in evidence at the 'night of the Maenads,' which gained some notoriety as the only time at which the revels of the conference came close to getting out of hand. From all accounts, the noise was the major disturbance, and rose to such a pitch that the neighbours (who were not exactly next door to such an estate) complained and even called in the local police. Jung himself was running around, making toasts, embracing the women, laughing his uproarious laugh, and baptising a few with libations of wine. A Dionysian revelry to be sure.

It lasted all night, but no description is available of the condition of the revellers the following morning. One hopes they did not have to listen to lectures all day. Perhaps all negative memories were lost as people recalled the great man really loosening up and letting go for the evening.

If Jung once more had the good fortune to receive from a woman as much or more than he gave, he also found Olga extremely useful in another way. Over the years, as an adjunct to Jungian analysis, a technique was developed by Jung known as 'active imagination'. Simply defined, this is a process in which material and images from dreams and fantasies are pictured in the mind's eye and then allowed to unfold with little or no conscious urging. In this way, the analysand very often gets the opportunity to work out unfinished dreams that are still troublesome, to see what unexpressed fantasies are present in the unconscious and to dialogue with previously unconscious material. In his essay on the process, Jung gives many warnings concerning the dangers of the technique and the need for the guiding hand of an analyst. For many, however, the dangers could not even be imagined for they were unable to do it at all. According to Dr Joseph Henderson, people who were stuck in their inability to relate to the unconscious would be sent to Frau Frobe-Kapteyn by Jung. She was highly intuitive and almost mediumistic and when these people would come to her from Jung she wouldn't *do* a thing. They would just sit in the room with her and spontaneously begin to have an active imagination. 'It happened to me once in her house. I just suddenly began to have visions!'[5]

Eranos is now entering into its fifty-seventh year and survives beyond the passing of the white-haired dynamic woman who evolved the vision from her intellectual isolation and the man who provided the catalyst. That Jung valued it is evident from a stone sculpture he commissioned from Paul Speck, which was erected in the garden of Eranos, and which bears the following inscription in Latin as a token of Jung's gratitude: 'to the Unknown Genius of this place.'

Notes

1. Dr Joseph Henderson, author's interview, November 1977.
2. B. Hannah, *Jung; His Life and Work*.
3. I. Progroff, *Spiritual Disciplines, Papers from the Eranos Yearbooks* 4.
4. A. Jaffé, *The Life and Work of C.G. Jung*.
5. Dr Liliane Frey-Rohn, author's interview, June 1978.
6. Dr Joseph Henderson, author's interview, November 1977.

CHAPTER TWELVE

Dion Fortune: Priestess

Most of the Jungian women either stayed close to Jung or visited him frequently as a way of renewing the spiritual link to him. One woman who admired his work tremendously and found in his writings the intellectual basis for the life path she chose, yet who never met him, was Dion Fortune. A ritual magician who continues to have a great influence on the development of English metaphysical thought, she is worth including as an example of a woman who read and assimilated Jung's works, but applied them to a field other than psychology.

Little is known of this controversial Englishwoman who, like the true magician she was, caused her personal effects and papers to be destroyed at her death. Born Violet Firth on 6 December 1890 in Wales, she later chose the Firth family motto, 'Deo non Fortuna' as her magical name and later, as her pen name.

In the earlier part of this century, education for women was a rarity and Violet, or Dion as we shall call her throughout this chapter, did not have a classical education, but had a very keen mind. Her interest in psychology seems to have come from attending classes at the University of London given by a Professor Flugel who as well as being a psychologist was also president of the Society for Psychical Research. She appears to have received a basic education in psychology and related subjects. She was particularly taken with Freud, Adler and Jung. Her main initial interest was in Freud and she was later to call herself a Freudian lay analyst when she worked in a clinic. However, the tenets of Jung gradually began to make more sense to her, especially in the light of her growing interest in Eastern philosophies and magic.

75

A friend from the time reports it this way: ' . . . she saw quite exceptionally clearly the close connection between modern empiricism and tried and tested tenets of Tantric and Qabbalistic ritualists . . . of the part played by the ancestral subconscious in the formation of character and personality. . . . '[1]

Another source perhaps states it more clearly: ' . . . psychology for Violet was the Outer Court, as she would come to express it. It was her means of making magic acceptable to the world at large – . . . it enabled her, she felt, to justify the philosophy and practise of magic, and to draw the right sort of (intelligent) people toward the enchanted circle in which she now found herself, outside of which she never stepped.'[2] Dion herself writes: 'And through all my experiences I was learning to interpret occultism in the light of psychology and psychology in the light of occultism, the one counterchecking and explaining the other.'[3]

During this time, she had a dream which changed the direction of her life: ' . . . she saw herself reading in the library of the Theosophical Society headquarters in London. As she raised her eyes from her books, a section of the wall solid with books and shelves faded away revealing a stairway out into space.'[4] She followed this stairway as the building disappeared and finally came to a place where three great figures were standing. They were ' . . . a blend of columns of pulsating and moving force represented as coloured lights and shaped into a semblance of humanoid form.'[5] From her studies she realised that one of them represented the forces of Nature, one the devotional path, and the other the hermetic or magical path. She was given to understand in the dream that hers was the hermetic path, or path of the intellect, but that she would need the balance of the other two in order to achieve her work. She was profoundly affected by this dream and made it the cornerstone for her life's task.

It was about this time that she 'looked at my psycho-analytical work straight in the face, and knew that I could no longer go on with it, threw up my post and joined the ranks of the Land Army.'[6] She had become aware in her therapeutic work that psychology did not have enough answers to satisfy her. This attitude may have been one of the reasons which prevented her from going to Jung and becoming another one of the women in the circle. Another was the fact that she was too much her own person to follow the tenets of another, even if the other was a genius. This was possibly a stroke of luck for her as Jung would certainly have objected to her examining 'occultism in the light of psychology and psychology in the light of occultism'. He took great pains for most of his career that no 'taint' of occultism touch him and that his psychology should be rooted in scientific thought. At least one of his biographers has taken him to task for this and demonstrated clearly the influence that paranormal experiences had on all his work and thought.[7] However in another sense Dion Fortune's work, despite being expressed in a very different language (magical as opposed to psychological), is heavily influenced by Jung.

'She felt as one of her tasks, the duty to put right the sexual interflow between man and woman, not merely on the physical plane, but on the inner-planes as well.'[8] She frequently states in her fictional as well as non-fictional works that the inner nature of woman was dynamic and the inner nature of man was passive and that on the inner-planes it was the woman who activated the man. This sounds a great deal like the anima-animus theory of Jung. In fact this work became one of the great tasks for her magical master plan. If they could have got past the difference in language, Jung and Fortune would have had much to say to one another. One feels that Dion could have done this, but that it would have been more difficult, if not impossible, for Jung.

There are many other echoes of Jung's ideas in those of Dion. Not that she got them from him necessarily, for she was following a parallel if difficult path. In *Psychic Self-Defense*, for example, she writes of the ' . . . mind side of nature, invisible to our senses, intangible to our instruments of precision . . . there are beings that live in this invisible world as fish live in the sea. There are also times when, as happens to a land when the sea-dykes break,

the invisible forces flow in upon us and swamp our lives.'⁹
This sounds very much like Jung's concept of the collective unconscious and the idea that autonomous complexes
reside there which can occasionally overwhelm us.

But it is when she writes about the relationship between
man and woman (and her ideas in this respect were sadly
out of tune with her own, and perhaps with our time,
too), that she seems in harmony with the psychology of
Jung. 'There is a commonplace relationship which you
can have with any female of the species, and there is a
subtle, magical relationship which is very rare. . . . The
knowledge of the subtle, magnetic relationship . . . People
think that sex is physical and that love is emotional and
they don't realise that there is something else between a
man and a woman which is magnetic in just the same
way as the compass turns to the pole . . . and it belongs
to Nature.'¹⁰

One wonders just what might have happened if these
two had met, and just what the effect on Jung's work
might have been. It is interesting to speculate that Jung,
who was a voracious reader of English mysteries and who
had been greatly impressed by H. Rider Haggard's book
She, might have read one of Dion's occult thrillers, such as
Sea Priestess, Moon Magic and others, which were fictional
accounts of her thought and her magical practices and an
important aspect of her work. Alas, we shall never know,
as few outside his family who knew him as a younger
man are now alive. And Dion's papers are gone.

Dion founded the Society of the Inner Light around or
before the early 1920s. This was a magical society of such
strength that it has lasted, though greatly changed, to this
day. The magical work she did there was intended to
influence the direction of society at that time, as she
realised the importance of bringing the Feminine back
into the world to balance to Masculine. A similar trend
is reflected in her work on the relationship between men
and women and in her later work which harked back to
Anthurian and Grail themes. In the later years of the
Society but during her lifetime, a reading of *The Psychology
of C.G. Jung* by Jolande Jacobi was required by novices,

demonstrating perhaps that she still felt the necessity for a psychological basis for her magical work.

Dion Fortune died in January, 1946 at only 55 years of age after the rapid onset of a form of leukaemia. She is buried in Glastonbury.

Notes

1. Quoted from an article by Bernard Bromage in *Light*, Spring 1960, courtesy of the College of Psychic Studies, as cited in A. Richardson, *Priestess*.
2. A. Richardson, *Priestess*.
3. D. Fortune, *Psychic Self-Defense*.
4. C. Fielding and C. Collins, *The Story of Dion Fortune*.
5. Ibid.
6. A. Richardson, *Priestess*.
7. C. Wilson, *Lord of the Underworld: C.G. Jung and the Twentieth Century*.
8. C. Fielding and C. Collins, *The Story of Dion Fortune*.
9. D. Fortune, *Psychic Self-Defense*.
10. D. Fortune, *The Sea Priestess*.

CHAPTER THIRTEEN

The Rest of the Entourage

Barbara Hannah: The Daughter of the Cathedral Close

It was reading Jung's essay, *Women in Europe*, in a magazine published in 1928, that brought Barbara Hannah to Zurich. She had been born almost forty years before, in 1891, in Brighton, England where her father was the first Vicar of Brighton, then Dean of Chichester, then Bishop. Most of her life before going to Zurich had been spent in the close of an Anglican cathedral, apart from some years spent in Paris studying art.

As a character, she stands out almost as much as Jacobi, though in a different way. She was always very much in evidence around Jung and cold-shouldered many others who wished to get close themselves. Mary Bancroft reports that she was '. . . a large English spinster of indeterminate age with a prominent nose that curved down to a chin that curved up to meet it . . . reminded me of the witch I had seen as a child in a production of Hansel and Gretel at the Boston Opera House. She was always making "in" jokes about arcane matters and laughing uproariously at certain obscure connections that puzzled me. She appeared oblivious of my existence and I felt even to comment about something as harmless as the weather would only increase the desolation of the Siberia to which she had apparently exiled me, thus defeating all attempts to establish contact.'[1]

In all descriptions of her she comes across as the almost archetypal English spinster, rather like a supporting character in the Agatha Christie thrillers of which Jung was so fond. One of her claims to fame within the Jungian group was that she was looked upon as Jung's greatest

80

miracle, as she was such an 'animus hound' (aggressive) when she arrived that she put everyone at a distance except Jung upon whom she doted. Jung managed to divert this energy into work which then became analysis, writing and eventually, teaching at the Institute.

Originally, Hannah had wanted to be a painter, but she felt that there were already enough paintings in the world and on reading Jung's article in Paris, she made up her mind to see him. In Zurich, she did a pencil sketch of Jung for his sixtieth birthday, but when sometime later she asked him where it was, he confessed he didn't know. She sensed he had rejected it and so felt no further desire to draw. When she talked it over with Jung at a later date, he felt that forgetting where it was was his unconscious way of leading her to a new direction of her energies which became her writing.[2]

Her classes at the Institute were concerned mainly with the Shadow, an apt subject for one who terrorised Mary Bancroft and others, and were extremely informative, if a bit on the dramatic side. She also came to all of her roommate von Franz's lectures and kept a watch to announce the time for breaks and for the end of the class. Von Franz would be deep in the realms of fairy-tales and Hannah would bring her back to earth abruptly by announcing the time.

Hannah wrote various books on analytical psychology, but perhaps one of her more lasting claims to fame is her biography of Jung. At once chatty and informative, this is one of the more personal books on him, and only in a few places does it smack of hero worship. But if she can occasionally be cloying, she can also let some of Jung's less endearing qualities be seen in a subtle way.

Hannah always felt she would live no longer than Jung's age at his own death (eighty-five), which perhaps showed the depth of her attachment and dependency. She died in 1986, however, at the age of ninety-five. Jung's greatest miracle repaid her debt to him.

Mary Foote's Notes

'Jung doesn't remove your complexes and he thinks all progress comes from conflict so, I suppose, one will go on conflicting for the rest of one's life.' This excerpt from a letter to Mabel Dodge Luhan makes Mary Foote sound weary and discouraged. It was most probably the discouragement one occasionally feels when one is far from home and hard at work in unfamiliar surroundings. Mary Foote never returned home until she was in her nineties.

Foote was a portrait painter of some note and in her studio at Number Three, Washington Square in New York City, and after the First World War, she brought together some of the brightest lights in the art and entertainment world of New York. She was a close friend of Robert Edmond Jones, the set designer, and it was Jones' letters from Zurich, where he went to consult with Jung, which were instrumental in bringing Foote there later. She was also a close friend of Mabel Dodge Luhan, the painter and author from Taos, New Mexico, friend of D.H. Lawrence, and of Henry James. She had also known Mark Twain in her childhood.

Much information about her years in Zurich is contained in her letters to Mabel Dodge Luhan. However, the journey that took her to Zurich was first to take her all round the world. It was Christmas 1926 when she left New York to sail for Peking, where she remained for four months. All the previous year she had corresponded with Jones while the latter was in Zurich.

Whilst in Peking something quite traumatic happened which caused her to write to Jung for help. His reply would suggest that she asked if it were any use going into analysis at the age of fifty-four:

Dear Miss Foote,

I rather prefer to have you come to Zurich about the middle of October [1927] for the Winter term. Age is of no importance. As long as you live, you have the problems of the living, only different ones that with 20.

Sincerely yours,

C.G. Jung

We have an idea of the trauma that led her to write to Jung in the following memoir by Mary Bancroft: ' . . . the novelist Ann Bridge had put her in a novel called *Peking Picnic* and the shock of seeing herself portrayed in a way she had never seen herself as being, had caused her to come to Zurich to consult Jung. I was told in this connection that a "sudden confrontation with the shadow" could be devastating.'¹

Foote arrived in Switzerland after coming across China by the Trans-Siberian Express, then the Orient Express to Marseilles, reaching Zurich in July 1927, a little sooner than Jung had suggested. Her stay was only brief, but she returned in January 1928, remaining there for the next twenty-five years.

Foote found the same conditions that all foreign visitors experienced then, as now, in greater or lesser degree. 'It's no use unless you can face considerable difficulty of one kind or another. In the first place, the isolation and gray damp weather of Zurich and the amount of time it takes to batter through at our age, and the probability of a not-particularly-thrilling collection of people to play with . . . ' She goes on to warn Luhan that she might not like the humble conditions, and much of the letter is an exaggeration, perhaps to keep Luhan from coming to Zurich. However, all of what she says can be too true, especially for the solitary tourist. The next part sounds like her true feelings without exaggeration. 'I wake up with the horrors frequently, but it isn't as bad as when I was trying to pay my way in New York . . . ' It is startling to realise that at that time Zurich was a cheaper place to live than New York!

The next letter gives an indication of the thing that was to keep her in Zurich the rest of her active life. 'There are a few people here whom I like, but I am living the most utterly monastic, hard-working life, sitting in the same spot day after day . . . I am interested and working hard . . . not much painting now – but doing some writing, *arranging notes for Jung* [italics mine] not original or to be published or anything, but exceedingly instructive and good for me'.

These notes, which she refers to as 'nothing important', were to become some of the most important work done for Jung. They are the notes of the Seminars on Analytical Psychology, better known as the English Seminars conducted by Jung for his English-speaking students, patients and colleagues for the years from 1929 to 1939. Although they cannot be published in book form since they were neither written nor edited for publication by Jung, they have been used by the succeeding generations of students at the Institute, and are exceedingly useful in the interpretation of symbolic material.

Mary Foote paid out of her own meagre pocketbook to have these notes copied and sent to subscribers throughout the United States and Europe. There were never more than 100 subscribers, so obviously most of the cost of printing and mailing was paid for by her. In those days women tended to do things like that without a second thought. Mary Foote was able to work closely with Jung as he went over the notes and perhaps she considered it well worth her time and money.

Even when the seminars were discontinued because of the war, Foote made it her life's work to edit them and eliminate all errors. She continued to do this right into her old age.

In the 1950s, Foote became increasingly senile. Another American woman, Mary Briner, who had stayed and become an analyst, brought her home to America, where she died in a Connecticut nursing home in 1968 at ninety-six.

Hilde Kirsch: The Exile

Many of the women who were admirers of Jung were, for one reason or another, not around him for as long as some of the others, either because they were married, or because they went back to their home countries periodically and then returned again and again for renewal. One such was Hildegard (Hilde) Kirsch, a Jungian analyst based in Los Angeles who died in 1978.

The night I interviewed her, the elements were raging outside her house in preparation for one of the worst floods in the history of Los Angeles. There were times that night when I had to ask her to repeat things as her voice was soft and still accented, and the noise of the storm all but drowned her out. I had been told she was ill, but when I saw her, I saw only a white-haired woman of average height, a spark still burning in her eyes, and I was not aware of any signs of physical weakness as we sipped sherry and talked. Such was her inner vitality that I did not know that she was suffering from a fatal illness and had but a few months to live.

She had been born in Germany, in a wealthy Jewish family, and had led an enviable life of ease until the First World War. When that was over she had lost a father and life became more difficult. She married and had two children, but her husband contracted a fatal disease and died, and the rise of Hitler forced her to leave Germany with her children for Palestine in 1935. She wrote a letter to Jung, asking if she might work with him that Spring. He wrote back that he was much too busy just then and she would have to wait for a year. After having lost her husband and given up much in her flight from Germany, she felt that a year later would not do at all. She decided, for the first time in her life, to consult the I Ching. It advised her, in the changing line, that she should 'cross the water to see the Great Man'. Even though her life was on the line so close to Nazi Germany, she took the next boat for Europe.

Once there, she went to Zurich and moved into a *pension* and there met a woman who was having an analysis with Jung. The next morning the woman summoned Hilde to her room and asked her to telephone Jung and tell him she was too ill to come and please cancel her appointment. She telephoned and insisted on speaking to Jung himself who did not like using the telephone. After giving him the message, she told him who she was, that the I Ching had told her to come, and that she wanted that appointment that had just become available. Jung roared with laughter and told her to come. She took the appointment and found that he had been telling the truth in his letter: he was booked all day long. Her future appointments had to be at seven o'clock in the morning.

Because of the way that Jung and his psychology changed her life, and because of his advice, she felt impelled to become an analyst herself and share his particular method with the world. She studied for a time in Zurich, then she met and married another German refugee and analyst, Dr James Kirsch. Together they went to England with her children. There, in London, they were part of a group that formed the Medical Society for Analytical Psychology. However, Hitler came ever closer, France fell, and they decided to go to America. By this time they had survived over 100 air raids in London and the journey by boat through U-boat infested waters did not seem any more dangerous than what they had already experienced. They settled in Los Angeles and helped to found the C.G. Jung Analytical Psychology Club there, and later, the Los Angeles C.G. Jung Institute.

Fourteen years after taking leave of Jung, she returned to Zurich. When she entered his consulting room, she looked at all the things that had been there when she had first seen him. As if he had read her thoughts, he said, 'Yes, Hilde. Everything is just the same'. This was reassurance on a deep level. Then they sat down and he picked up with the dream she had had when she last saw him, fourteen years and a world war before. As one whose life had been turned upside down several times, Hilde needed a feeling of continuity, and Jung had provided it in a simple, caring way.

Hilde spoke of a dream she had that was embarrassing to her, and which she felt foolish telling him, of being his bride. He replied that in a way the dream was true, for she was a Taurus and he had his moon in Taurus which matched them astrologically. The embarrassment eased for her and she felt healed by his response. In general Jung was careful with the feelings of the women and was very conscious of the effect he had on them.

Hilde Kirsch's career ended with her death in 1978 after almost forty years as an analyst. This was only a few weeks after our interview.

Mary Bancroft: The Spy Who Loved Him

Mary Bancroft, though she was close to Jung for a long time, was never one of the women who were constantly around him. Perhaps one of the things that kept her separate was that she was married (to a Swiss banker) and had an independent career as a journalist.

This remarkable woman was born in Massachusetts in 1903, to the family that published the Wall Street Journal. After a second marriage she moved to Zurich, where her husband had his business, in the early 1930s. Strangely enough, she had been considering going there to consult with Jung on a problem which concerned 'sneezing fits' that she suspected were psychosomatic.

She was beautiful, sexy and intelligent, very vivacious and interested in everything. Once in Zurich, she went to a series of lectures that Jung was giving at the Eidengenoss-ische Technische Hochschule to see what he was like before she made a commitment to therapy. 'I do remember how tremendously impressed I was by him. Although he was twenty-eight years older than I, I found him extremely attractive as a man. This was a shock. Until that moment I had never regarded men more than at most ten years older than myself as "sex objects". But what impressed me most was his perfectly extraordinary wit, so rare in a person of his vast erudition.'[1]

From those lectures, she went to the English seminars, then into analysis with Toni Wolff, and finally she had a four-year analysis with Jung. During this time, she was at least able to relieve herself of her sneezing fits when she realised they were a reaction to a feeling she couldn't say 'no' to anyone for fear they wouldn't love her. She also rid herself of a writing block with Jung's help.

When the war broke out in Europe, Allen Dulles, who became head of the CIA, slipped into Switzerland just ahead of the Nazi march into France, sealing off the Swiss borders. Unable to bring any of his OSS agents into the country, he recruited people he met there for different tasks, among them Mary Bancroft. Her biggest worry was whether she could keep her mouth shut because she was such an extrovert. She went to Jung, telling him her worry. He said *he* thought she could do it, but added, 'Probably only the thought that 5000 people would be dead if you didn't would ever make you do it.' He also told her that doing such a job would probably reveal to her much more about herself, which she subsequently found to be true.

One of the things that she had to keep to herself was the fact that there was a conspiracy against Hitler by his officers and generals, and highly placed German civilians. The fact that Jung was in on the information with Dulles' knowledge should stop once and for all the persistent rumours that Jung was a Nazi 'sympathiser'.

Mary Bancroft stayed on in Switzerland until after the end of the Second World War, in constant touch with Jung. Eventually, she moved to New York where she was a staunch supporter of the C.G. Jung Institute.

On Jung's eightieth birthday she wrote to him, saying that she understood that in some tribes the chief would answer one question from each of his followers on his eightieth birthday. Her question, therefore, was, 'Have you ever seen a helpless woman, for I never have?' His answer was that a man's helplessness can be real, but 'a woman's was one of her best stunts. As she is by birth and sex on better terms with nature, she is never quite helpless as long as there is no man in the vicinity.'

Lucile Elliott: The Dreamer

'Jung really hurt my feelings.' Dr Lucile Elliott still felt that hurt when she was over eighty-five years old. She was speaking of the second time she had gone to Zurich to see Jung, who had given her analysis nineteen years earlier. Just prior to that second visit she had lost someone with whom she had had a twenty-six year long relationship. He had died and she had had a disturbing dream in which she had been lying in a coffin near the grave of her friend, and a tree was growing out of her forehead. In the dream she kept getting out of the coffin to go to her friend's grave. She had been profoundly disturbed by the dream, wondering whether it spoke of a desire to die or of a new life. She went back to Zurich to see the man who had helped her before. He refused to see her. He said that she was still too involved with him, and that he was too old to work it through with her. He was almost eighty. So, instead, she had an hour with Frau Jung who was very helpful and kind, but the hurt from Jung's refusal stayed with her.

Lucile Elliot began her career in general medicine. She had graduated from medical school at the University of California at Berkeley in 1924. By that time the suffragettes had won the vote and she found medical school to be without prejudice against her sex. Internships were given out based on grades, regardless whether one was male or female. She began her practice in Berkeley.

A few years after graduation she found herself in an 'intolerable situation which I couldn't take and couldn't leave alone', so she went into therapy with Dr Elizabeth Whitney, one of the first Jungian analysts in the San Francisco Bay area. After five years with her, she still felt she needed something else, so Dr Whitney sent her to Dr Jung in Zurich in 1935.

'He was the greatest man I ever met.' She had a six-month analysis with Jung and felt the healing take place over that period. Because she was so introverted, she remained in her hotel room most of the time, meeting no one except Barbara Hannah who was staying at the same hotel. 'When she [Hannah] entered the room, it was as if a dark shadow entered.'

Back in San Francisco, she felt her life had come together sufficiently for her to need no further analysis, but she didn't feel ready to be an analyst herself.

Three or four years later, Dr Joseph Wheelwright and his wife, who were both analysts, returned from Zurich and together with Elizabeth Whitney and Elliot, they formed the Society of Jungian Analysts of San Francisco.

A year or so later, the Second World War began and Dr Elliott once more had to postpone her practice as an analyst; too many doctors were being called into the Army and people in the United States were short of medical care. It wasn't until 1946, when doctors were finally returning to their practices, that Dr Elliott was able to give up general medicine and become a full-time analyst.

She continued to practice and see a few people into her late eighties though her eyesight was failing and she had a bad knee which forced her to live in a retirement home. All the wisdom of her rich life was in her face which continually crinkled into good humour.

The hurt from Jung? 'Oh, a few years ago I had a vision of Dr Jung rising from the depths of the water. He had on a black veil over him, covered with jewels all over. He had his same friendly smile, but now his hair was long and I could see that he looked like an old testament prophet. That healed the hurt.'

Notes

BARBARA HANNAH
1. M. Bancroft, '*Jung and his Circle*', in *Psychological Perspectives*, Autumn 1975.
2. '*The Introverted Jung, Conversations with Barbara Hannah*', *Psychological Perspectives*, Autumn-Winter, 1988.

MARY FOOTE
1. M. Bancroft, '*Jung and his Circle*', in *Psychological Perspectives*, Autumn 1975.

Much of the rest of this section comes from interviews and from an excellent article on 'Who was Mary Foote?' by E. Foote in *Spring*, 1974.

HILDA KIRSCH
All of this material comes from the author's interview in February 1978 with Mrs Kirsch at her home in Los Angeles shortly before her death.

MARY BANCROFT
1. M. Bancroft, '*Jung and his Circle*', in *Psychological Perspectives*, Autumn 1975.

THE REST OF THE ENTOURAGE

LUCILE ELLIOTT
This section came entirely from the author's interview with Dr Elliott at her home in February 1978.

CHAPTER FOURTEEN

The Times, Jung, and the Women

Jung was a man far ahead of the times in which he lived. So much was he a man of that overworked phrase, 'the Aquarian age', that it is easy to forget that he was actually born in 1875, just past the middle of the Victorian era.

Many of the charges levelled by women against his psychological writings are true: it is as full of patriarchal and chauvinistic attitudes as is almost all the literature of that age, although the chauvinism is more benevolent than that of, say, Freud.

As late as 1955, when he was eighty years old, he was still saying things like: 'A man's foremost interest should be his work. But a woman – man is her work and her business . . . a home is like a nest – not enough room for both birds at once. One sits inside, the other perches on the edge and looks about and attends to all outside interests.'[1]

Statements such as this often make women grind their teeth in fury. Deservedly. It makes no room for individual choices or needs. Interestingly enough, though he voiced many of the prejudices of his day, there is little indication that he used them to any real extent in his actual relationships with the women around him. Except that evidently his wife lived out his belief – she was at home the first twenty years of their married life, and, as we have seen, did not always like it. In addition, of course, he practised the double standard that was not uncommon in his day.

In spite of his public attitudes, he took women very seriously, something that came across repeatedly from the women I was able to interview. One pointed out to me that Jung's typology is non-sexist and helped women out of their Victorian prison. However, a recent writer makes a different case: 'He seemed surprised that women should think rather than feel, work rather than mother . . . '[2] And again, 'For instance in his general description of the various psychological types, Jung claims that introverted feeling is mainly to be found among women.'[3] This writer then goes on to make a point, which is the same as the one I would wish to make: 'I am not alone in having been struck by the discrepancies between these attitudes of Jung's . . . on the one hand, and on the other, the life in Zurich between the wars. In the sub-culture of analytical psychology at least, the city was home to several high-achieving women analysts. These women . . . do not appear to have felt any anxiety or conflict between their career orientation and what they had to say about being feminine.'[4]

The women came to Jung and seemed to thrive on whatever it was that he gave them in analysis and relationship. The exact nature of what it was varied from person to person. Part of it came certainly from their projections upon him of the genius, healer, great teacher, wise man. However, it is also certain that he gave these projections back to the women for them to integrate into their own psyches. If he had not, they would have never been able to write their books, teach their classes, or treat their patients.

To fully understand what was going on between Jung and the women, it is necessary to understand two things: what it was these women had in common, and the basis of Jung's attraction for them. Jung's own psychological writings will provide us with a useful tool for this.

First of all, what did the women have in common? One of the Jungian women *not* in the inner circle has pointed out that these women all had big animuses. Animus is a term used (confusedly at times) by Jungians to explain the more assertive or aggressive characteristics of women, which in turn are attributed to an inner masculine image. This term had a lot to do with what society did and did not feel to be women's natural instincts. Jung, instead of describing them as unfeminine traits, gave them all a catch-all word: animus. He said that there was both a positive and a negative aspect to the animus, but more often seems to regard it with fear and loathing: 'A woman should constantly control the animus: by undertaking some intellectual work', 'Many a woman has been driven to disaster by her animus'; and finally, 'If a woman dreams of a superior role she wishes to assume in the world, it is best to advise her to write an essay or an article about her wishes . . . '[5]

According to one woman Jungian analyst, 'With Jung, for the first time the animus had a place to go, so he attracted all these women with whopping great animuses and the rest wound up in booby hatches ordinarily. In my day it was "never let the animus out when a man is around".'[6]

Many of the women who came to him, such as Bertine, Mann and Harding were already professionals, but theirs was a lonely way. Many others had simply stifled their ambitions and channelled them into inappropriate but socially acceptable areas. We still see such women today who drive their husbands and children to hypertension with their own swallowed ambitions and aggressions. If they have no husbands or children in whom they can live out these drives, they often tend to put their energies into negative relationships with any people with whom they continually come into contact. Most of the women who came to Jung did so because they were neurotic. To what extent this was because they were ambitious and aggressive, we can only guess. It is at least possible that whatever problems they had were made worse by the lack of outlet for their enormous talents and energies.

Some had university training and others had little or no formal education, but most of them came from cultured backgrounds. They were mostly upper class, no matter what country they came from. This is easily explained by the fact that only the upper classes and intellectuals travelled in those days. It is only in the last forty years that foreign travel, other than for immigration or military purposes, has spread to the other classes.

Perhaps the most revealing common feature of the women was that most of them, with only one or two exceptions, remained unmarried. Being unmarried is a valid choice today, particularly in the middle and upper classes. However, in the first fifty or sixty years of this century, when they were not looked upon as jokes or family drudges, unmarried women were regarded with pity and sometimes even suspicion. Only in England were they treated with anything like respect, and then only if they spent their days performing useful duties in church or family.

Most of the women, therefore, were unmarried, intelligent, talented and upper class, possibly with a profession, and troubled.

We must now see what sort of man it was who was able to provide each of them with what she needed to live a long, creative and full life.

Notes

1. 'Men, Women and God', a condensation of interviews with Jung by Frederick Sands in W. McGuire and R.F.C. Hull (eds), *C.G. Jung Speaking: Interviews and Encounters.*
2. A. Samuels, *Jung and the Post-Jungians.*
3. Ibid.
4. Ibid.
5. Ibid.
6. M. Ostrowski-Sachs, *Conversations with C.G. Jung.*

CHAPTER FIFTEEN

Jung: the Animus Mundi

One thing became apparent in the writing of this book: Jung's need for the women was as great as theirs for him. I have shown how his relationship to his mother, Emilie Preiswerk Jung, laid the basis for his relationship to women in general, and to those in his circle in particular: it created within him a lifelong need for the intellectual and creative companionship of women. The need seems of a size proportionate to his gifts, and was not simply the desire of most men to be admired by women, although that was certainly present.

Even in his near-death experience, it was his connection to the women that had a great deal to do with his survival. In the midst of it, the doctor who was treating him floated up to him in a vision. The phantom doctor explained to Jung that he wouldn't be allowed to die because at least thirty women were too upset at the idea of his leaving them and his work.

Jung's was a deep psychic need on which his creativity and the wholeness of his psyche was dependent. It was no accident that he chose a woman to accompany him on his journey into the depths of his own unconscious, who thereby became Carl Jung's analyst: Toni Wolff. For him, women and the unconscious were synonymous. He had said that if men made an infantile resistance to women, they were also resisting their own unconscious side.

In his writing, as we have seen, he shows less understanding and more of the prejudices of his age than in his actual therapeutic and personal contact with women, perhaps because he was using his thinking function and not his feeling. His written statements show his own needs: 'One should never be curious with women'[1] and 'Marriage is indeed a brutal reality, yet the experimentum crucis of life. I hope you learn to endure and not to struggle against the necessities of fate. Only thus you remain in the centre.'[2] This closely echoes the feelings he expressed about the hold on reality which Emma and his children provided him when he made his plunge into unknown psychological territory. The contradictory image becomes less so when we see that for Jung woman represented psychic totality: both the vital link to the unconscious and the hold on daily reality. Personally speaking, she was his Emma, but she was also Toni, and perhaps even Linda, Jolande, Barbara, Esther, Eleanor, Mary and so on.

It was his overwhelming need for women that provided him with his gift of understanding them to such an extent that he seemed almost to create them. Given the calibre of women who came to him, perhaps 'free' and 'evoke' are more accurate words. It became apparent over and over again in the interviews and the research that the women involved all felt he had saved their lives. Perhaps this was an expression of a psychic component within himself of which he was largely unconscious: the image of Pygmalion. In his *Collected Works* almost every other mythological theme had at least a passing reference. Pygmalion is conspicuous by its absence.

The myth of Pygmalion has been somewhat debased in its rendering by that noted misogynist, Bernard Shaw. His *Pygmalion* was an arrogant pedagogue named Professor Higgins, who, to show his basic contempt for society is valid, makes a bet that he can get a very lower-class flower woman accepted into society simply by refining her speech and deportment. Once he had accomplished this superficial change, he himself fell in love with her.

The original Greek myth has little to do with this reworked version. It tells how Pygmalion was a sculptor who created a statue of Love herself – Aphrodite – as woman. He then proceeded to fall in love with his own creation. So piteously did he beg the goddess to come alive and dwell within the statue, that Aphrodite caused

the statue to become flesh and blood in the form of Galatea. From the union of Galatea and Pygmalion came a
son who was first of a line of kings of Cyprus, where the
goddess herself dwelt and where her worship had its ori-
gins. In Jung, we have a man who was a worshipper, on
a psychic level, of the goddess. In an unpublished letter
to Mary Foote, postmarked Cyprus, 1933, he wrote, 'Here
are some greetings from the enchanted island of roses;
more than that – *here I found a piece of my spiritual ancestry*'.[3]

He seemed to have an uncanny knack of seeing in each
woman who came to him her true gifts and talents, and
an even more useful talent, that of evoking these gifts.
The process must have seemed like the old magic technique, used by secret lodges and societies throughout the
ages, of creating a magical image. Dion Fortune gives us
a good description in one of her popular magic novels. It
is a dialogue between a man and the woman who is trying
to become a priestess of the sea goddess in this century:

' "The next step", said she, staring into the fires and not looking
at me, "is to complete my own training."
"That being?" said I.
"To make the magical image of myself as a sea-priestess. A
magical image does not exist on this plane at all. It is in another
dimension, and we make it with imagination. As for that, I
need help for I cannot do it alone. For me to make a magical
image of myself is auto-suggestion and this begins and ends
subjectively. But when two or three of us work together, and you
picture me as I picture myself, then things begin to happen." '[4]

I have quoted verbatim because I feel it describes the
Pygmalion-like technique that Jung employed, to what
extent consciously, I do not know. Jung saw something
in the women in analysis that either they did not see
themselves until he saw it, or that they had had evoked
by him. Perhaps often they could not see it for fear of
ridicule for being an 'uppity' woman who dares to think
that she has a serious contribution to make. Once he saw
it, and provided through his psychology and its associated
functions a way of using these talents, the women blos-
somed. This might be one of the most important reasons

they had for protecting the safe space he provided and guarding it jealously from newcomers until these proved themselves permanent, and from the public in general. There were not many such places for intellectual women in those days outside the universities, and in many cases they were not welcome even there.

It is true that in keeping them safe and protected, Jung was also surrounding himself with admirers, but if that had been all there was to it these gifted women would not have remained long, nor added yearly to their numbers. He continued to nourish and his psychology had its roots in something real.

In addition being something of a Pygmalion figure, Jung also fulfilled other roles, wittingly and unwittingly. One of the strongest was that of shaman or medicine-man to his 'tribe'.

Being a shaman is different to being a priest. A priest is always tied to the society in which he lives. If he delivers the word of the gods or the unconscious, he also gives that of society and its expectations. Almost always he is seen as the intermediary between the gods and humankind. The shaman, on the other hand, is the loner; the one who seeks out his own way in the wilderness of the human condition and takes no one else's word for what the gods say, nor for what they are. If he has followers, he often passes on spiritual truths he has learned himself, but also encourages them to have their own experiences of the divine. In Joseph Campbell's words: ' . . . the shaman is one who, as a consequence of a personal psychological crisis, has gained a certain power of his own.'⁵ Jung's own plunge into the psyche certainly gave him an authority no amount of education could have done.

Dr Joseph Henderson has spoken of the uncanny side of Jung's nature which at times made him appear almost frightening. He described it as Jung's shamanistic side which endowed him with the kind of intuition which could go right to the heart of a person's troubles with great perception.

This brings up another facet of Jung's attractiveness:

the uncanny way he had of coming right to the heart of something without consciously seeming to know what was wrong. One doctor I interviewed even spoke of Jung being 'unconscious' and operating from that level. Dr Liliane Frey-Rohn first met Jung at a party when he came up to her, put his hand on her back and said, 'This is where your soul is'. It was so much the truth for her that she contacted him soon after for analysis.

Jung himself describes how he was asked by another doctor to see a young woman whom the doctor had not been able to help and who was, seemingly, beyond help. The woman showed up as arranged to see Jung and he spent an hour with her. During this time, an old nursery rhyme came into his head and he began to sing it. The hour soon came to an end and she left. He did not hear anything more of her or her case until years later when a doctor came over to him and introduced himself as the doctor who had sent the young woman to him, many years before. He asked Jung what 'miracle' he performed with her, for she had come home completely cured and was even now leading a normal life.[6]

Over and over again we have stories of Jung's ability to 'read minds'. Renée Brand told a story of how she and ten students from the Institute were invited to the planting of a tree at Jung's home on his eightieth birthday. She noticed how frail he was, and as the gardeners were digging a hole for the tree, she began to have an awareness of a more sinister implication for the hole. Suddenly Jung was beside her and telling her that it was not a burial but the planting of new life.

Another author writes: 'The main talent of the shaman is that of throwing himself into a trance at will . . . and it is while in this trance that he performs his miraculous deeds.'[7]

Because of this ability to virtually mind read, he met his patients at a very deep level. And it is no wonder that the women speak of 'miracles' at times. In a world where there is so much talk about communication, but where there is still so little of it, to be met at this level and by someone who answers questions without one ever needing

to ask them does indeed seem miraculous. 'The
shaman . . . is not only a familiar denizen, but even a
favoured scion, of those realms of power that are invisible
to our normal waking consciousness, which all may visit
briefly in vision, but through which he roams, a master.'[8]
Another common projection on Jung was that of the
Wise Old Man of Bollingen Tower. When his name is
mentioned now, the picture it evokes is that of the white-
haired old man of later years. As Barbara Hannah wrote
in her biography of Jung: ' . . . his school fellows at the
gymnasium already called him "Father Abraham".'[9]

He had seemed too old for his years from an early age
and, while still a child, was aware of a part of himself
that was a wise old man. He writes of how, aged twelve
and the guest of some friends of the family, he frightened
his host by standing up in the back of a boat for which
he received a dressing-down. 'I was thoroughly crestfallen
and had to admit that I had done exactly what he had
asked me not to do, and that his rage was quite justified.
At the same time I was seized with rage that this fat,
ignorant boor should dare to insult ME. This ME was
not only grown up, but important, an authority, a person
with office and dignity, an object of respect and awe.'[10]

This aspect of Jung was particularly noticeable to
people who met him in later years. Elizabeth Ostermann
told me that the force that came from him was incredible,
that he seemed very powerful and aware of his power,
although in no way would he misuse it.[11]

Perhaps he did not become fully aware of this part of
his psyche until he went into his dark night of the soul
and began to have visions. The first character in those
visions was Elijah. 'The atmosphere was that of another
world. Near the steep slope of a rock I caught sight of
two figures, an old man with a white beard and a beautiful
young girl. I summoned up my courage and approached
them as I thought they were real people. . . . The old
man explained that he was Elijah and that gave me a
shock. . . . Soon after this fantasy another figure arose out
of the unconscious. He developed out of the Elijah figure.
I called him Philemon.'[12] Philemon appeared to him as a

'winged being sailing across the sky. I saw that it was an old man with the horns of a bull. He held a bunch of four keys. . . . He had the wings of a kingfisher with its characteristic colours.'[13]

Much later in life he was able to say: 'At Bollingen I am in the midst of my true life. I am most deeply myself. Here I am, as it were, the "age-old son of the Mother". That is how alchemy puts it very wisely, for the "old man", the "ancient", whom I had already experienced as a child, is personality number two, who has always been and always will be. He exists outside of time and is the son of the maternal unconscious.'[14] He had integrated Philemon so well that he seemed to have become him: the shamanistic, mediumistic, old wise man.

Notes

1. From a letter to Jolande Jacobi, 20 November 1928. G. Adler (ed.) *C.G. Jung: Letters*, Volume 1 1906–50.
2. From a letter to an anonymous correspondent, 29 September 1934, Ibid.
3. E. Foote, 'Who was Mary Foote?', *Spring*, 1974.
4. D. Fortune, *The Sea Priestess*.
5. J. Campbell, *Flight of the Wild Gander*.
6. C.G. Jung, *Memories, Dreams, Reflections*.
7. J. Campbell, *Flight of the Wild Gander*.
8. Ibid.
9. B. Hannah, *Jung: His Life and Work*.
10. C.G. Jung, *Memories, Dreams, Reflections*.
11. Interview with the author, November 1977.
12. C.G. Jung, *Memories, Dreams, Reflections*.
13. Ibid.
14. Ibid.

CHAPTER SIXTEEN

The Valkyries: an Assessment

Most of the first generation of the women who knew Jung intimately and worked with him are dead, and only one or two remain. Perhaps it is easier now to assess clearly the contribution these women have made to society in general and to Jungian psychology in particular.

The first, most obvious point is that all their work, particularly their therapy was and is done specifically in the context of Jungian psychology. To what degree they were 'good' analysts is impossible to know given the privileged information ethic of the psycho-analytical couch (or chair, in the case of the Jungians). We can only, therefore, assess them from their written work.

In the case of Emma Jung, given that the uncompleted manuscript of her major work, *The Grail Legend*, is unavailable to us in its pre-von Franz form, we can only assess her by her one completed work, *Anima and Animus*. This work largely restates Jung's ideas about his twin concept of the anima and the animus. She adds very little of her own, although her book is a little more readable than much of what Jung wrote, and of course, not so contradictory. I say 'of course' because many of Jung's contradictions came about as a result of the fifty-year period over which his work and theories developed and his perceptions changed. Emma Jung's essays were done in a much shorter time and rely heavily on her husband's work to date.

It is much the same with Antonia Wolff, who suffers from the added difficulty that much of her work remains unpublished in English, and what is published is poorly circulated. Again, from what little we know, her work is very much based on Jung's formulations and she did little of her own original research, except of a highly selected sort. Her much quoted psychological types of women, structured on those of Jung, are very patriarchal, and only see women in relation to men. Although her poetry was reputed to be excellent, none is to be found.

Linda Fierz-David also uses Jung's premises unquestioningly in her two major works, although we do occasionally get a personal sense of her, and her aesthetic sensibility is evident. How wonderful it would be if the fairy-tales that she wrote and illustrated for her children were published, as her son had wished. He spoke of doing so in my interview with him several years ago, but now he is dead.

In such women as Jolande Jacobi, Barbara Hannah, M. Esther Harding (with one exception, as we shall see) and Eleanor Bertine, the emphasis on an unquestioning use of Jungian constructs is particularly acute. Dr Jacobi made his psychology approachable to the general public (without much thanks, it seems), and we can be grateful to her. But in the other women's work, this unquestioning acceptance becomes very apparent as old themes from fairy-tales, myths and even the Brontës are fitted into the standard Jungian mold.

Upon reading the books of many of the Jungian women, all one finds is a re-hash of old and not necessarily tried and trusted Jungian formulations. Only the third generation of women seem to be breaking free from this. I have a hunch that Jung would have quickly become bored by much of what has been written, and would have looked in vain for a more questioning attitude. I particularly feel this should have been done with the concept of the animus, and only one woman, Irene Claremont de Castillejo, comes close to disputing with the master and acquits herself well in so doing.[1]

Scholars in other fields seem to be tiring of this unthinking acceptance. In an introduction to Max Luthi's *Once Upon A Time: On the Nature of Fairy-tales*, the folklorist Frances Lee reveals his impatience in the following paragraph: 'Depth psychology, the interpretation of the single tale in terms of some kind of Freudian or Jungian archetype, is a favourite method often practised in a mechanical manner and without paying any attention to the significance of the individual teller. "Psychological universals" like the great mother, the Oedipal drive, and the Cainite urge, submerge the individual psyche. And yet the human being who tells the story is quite as important to any ultimate hypothesis of archetype as a single folktale history is to the history of the genre. More so, indeed *if depth psychology is really interested in its proper subject matter, the living person.*'[2]

Some feminist scholars are asking why no Jungian women (nor many of the men for that matter, with the outstanding exception of James Hillman) have questioned Jung's ideas nor done much more than amplify *ad nauseam* his basic assumptions. Naomi Goldenberg, who herself attended the Jung Institute in Zurich at the same time I did, has written an excellent essay citing many cases of how the very subjective selection of research material is used to 'document preordained conclusions'.[3]

One exception to this slavish following the master is M. Esther Harding's *Women's Mysteries*, which is grounded in history as well as psychology. Moreover, her research served as the basis for many of the early goddess books that followed. As stated in Chapter Seven, it would seem that initially at least, Jung did not much care for it.

Apart from this, it may be stated that while the women around Jung were undoubtedly creative, intelligent women, none of them diverged very far from his thought, nor deepened it noticeably. Not one of them ever saw fit to question any of his assertions about women and the animus concept, nor added any conflicting research of her own. Certainly they would have been in a better position, if only because of their sex, to give empirical observations of their own and other women's psyches. Their observations on the animus would have been particularly valuable, but only if they had taken the liberty first of putting aside Jung's assumptions. He himself makes several statements throughout his writings concerning the nebulousness of his basic material on the animus, for example: 'Since the anima is an archetype that is found in men, it is reasonable to *suppose* (italics mine) that an equivalent archetype must be present in women'.[4] Reasonable to whom? Why not suppose that because man is born of 'other' (woman) that he must have reflection of her in his unconscious so as to help him subconsciously relate to the 'other', while woman is born of 'same' (woman) and does not have this need in the same way? Goldenberg notes that Jung's followers: 'are prone to emphasise (the anima-animus model) to an even greater degree than Jung himself'.[5] Of course, any woman maintaining too strongly that the concept of animus is erroneous is likely to be told that the mere fact that she challenges it is indication that she is animus possessed!

The one woman in our book who seems to have been pretty much her own person despite an admiration for Jung is Dion Fortune. She says little that is inimicable to his psychology, but writes without much use of psycho-jargon, and applies her ideas to the daily lives of men and women. Perhaps the very fact that she did not go to Zurich to undergo analysis helped her to keep her perspective.

The women around Jung might have been better advised to follow the advice from the *Collected Works*, Vol. 7: 'Therefore anyone who wants to know the human psyche would be better advised to bid farewell to his study and wander with the human heart through the world. There, in the horrors of prisons, lunatic asylums and hospitals, in drab suburban pubs, in brothels and gambling hells, in the salons of the elegant, the Stock Exchanges, socialist meetings, churches, spiritualist gatherings and ecstatic sects, through love and hate, through experience of passion in every form in his own body, he would reap richer store of knowledge than textbooks a foot thick could give him and he would know how to doctor the sick with a real knowledge of the human soul'.[6]

Notes

1. I. Claremont de Castillejo, *Knowing Woman*.
2. M. Luthi, *Once Upon A Time: On the Nature of Fairy-Tales*.

3. N. Goldenberg, '*A Feminist Critique of Jung*', in *Signs: The Journal of Women in Culture and Society*, Vol. 2 No. 2, 1976.
4. M. Ostrowski-Sachs, *Conversations with C.G. Jung.*
5. N. Goldenberg, '*A Feminist Critique of Jung*'.
6. *The Collected Works of C.G. Jung*, Vol. 7.

CHAPTER SEVENTEEN

The Hieros Gamos

The old alchemist stands amidst his tables covered with bubbling retorts and bottles of mysteriously coloured liquids. At his side, working with him each step of the way, is a young woman who goes about her work, occasionally checking with the old sage. There is a sense of tension in the air and a feeling that many more unseen beings are present in the ancient laboratory.

The alchemist has been working for many years at this one process, trying first one combination of ingredients, then another. Finally he is ready. All the carefully chosen components have gone into the athanor, that small furnace made for the working of the *magnum opus*. Essences of many plants, flowers and herbs are included. Today they put in the extract of sunlight; now tonight it will be the moon's silvery rays, and then the mixture should be ready!

The hands of the young woman tremble as she parts the curtains. It is the only sign that she is nervous. A full moon is temporarily hiding behind a wisp of night-blue clouds. Then slowly its silver beams of muted light shine into the room and deep into the open door of the athanor where the old man has placed it to receive the moon essence. He now adds a drop of something else as his *soror mystica*, the sister of his soul, looks on. The operation is complete. He quickly shuts the door and takes one final glance at the beloved woman who has worked so long beside him.

The athanor glows and turns red. Inside, the process has begun and there is no stopping it now save at the loss of everything. All night the process continues and it is only by the softened noises within the tightly shut furnace and the heat coming from it that one can tell that something is happening. There seems to be no one in the room to witness it. Both the old sage and the young woman have receded into the shadows where they wait, unseen even to each other.

Finally, there is a change in the athanor. It has ceased to glow or make noises of any kind. From out of the shadow comes a solitary figure; a tall, slender person who goes with youthful vigour straight to the small oven and unhesitatingly opens the door. The strong smooth hand reaches inside to draw out the substance, and as it does so a sinuous jewelled snake coils around the wrist until its head meets its tail, which it then puts in its mouth and seems to doze off. The hands withdraw the work, a work that would pass unnoticed by the uninitiated: a large, smooth stone. Just a stone, but within it are the opposites contained in eternal balance, rotating to a celestial rhythm so precisely tuned that to the untrained eye the effect is one of stasis.

The figure with its bracelet of jewelled serpent holds the stone reverently aloft and in the light that it gives off, we see that the figure is neither that of the old alchemist, nor of his young female helper. It is a being, complete in itself, neither male nor female, yet both, with all the wisdom of age, yet sustained by youthful vigour. The *magnum opus* has taken place. The androgynous being has been created through the *hieros gamos*.

*

The ultimate goal in Jungian analysis, or the process of individuation which it facilitates, is the *hieros gamos* or Divine Marriage. Jung borrowed the term from medieval alchemy and his last great work, *The Mysterium Coniunctionis*, was devoted to its study and psychological interpretation. This operation is so complex that it would take the volume Jung wrote to fully explain it. However, to put it (perhaps unfairly) in the simplest terms possible, the *hieros gamos* is the process whereby the attributes of Sol (masculine, sun) are brought together with those of Luna (feminine, moon), to create a single androgynous being.

Psychologically this process takes place within an individual when a man integrates his opposite and a woman integrates hers. At this point, each of them becomes psychologically androgynous: there is no further split within them. It is a marriage of the conscious and the unconscious. The resulting totality brings about a 'new' person: a psychic rebirth has taken place. Of course, it is the ideal; a life-enhancing vision of the possibilities of psychic union.

I believe that the women around Jung used their relationship with him to act out the *hieros gamos*. They felt 'married' to him at a very deep level, and perhaps this is part of the reason why most of them remained unmarried. It would be difficult for a 'mere' earthly man to compete with such a figure who reached these women in such a meaningful way for them. This theme shows up frequently: in Hilde Kirsch's dream and Jung's interpretation of it; in the dream of Jolande Jacobi; and even in the facetious nickname given to another of the women who idolised Jung and who was referred to as the 'bride of Christ'.

If we were to extend this premiss even further, we might say that the whole body of work that came from these women is the child or product of this union, which is perhaps why it takes so much from Jung and contains so little original thought and research.

Whatever the premiss, the life-sustaining nature of the deep union is shown in the long, productive lives of these women. In each case, their relationship with Jung enabled them to live their lives at a very deep level, and their dreams and visions sustained them beyond the death of the man who had taken them seriously for the first time.

APPENDIX

Jung's Birth Chart

'There are many analogies which can be made between the horoscope and the character disposition. There is even the possibility of certain predictive powers. . . . The horoscope seems to correspond to psychic archetypes.'[1]

'We are born at a given moment, in a given place, and we have, like the best wines, the quality of the year and the season which witness our birth. Astrology claims no more than this.'[2]

Carl Gustave Jung was born at the time when the Sun was in the sign of Leo and the Saturn-ruled sign of Capricorn was rising at the eastern horizon of his birthplace, Kesswil, Switzerland.

Astrologically, the rising sign indicates how the world sees and views the individual, as well as the way in which the individual tends to see, view and interact with his/her environment. The Sun indicates the Ego and the potential within the individual to continue to be and to become whatever it is the essence of that individual to be and become.

The Saturn-ruled sign of Capricorn portends early limitations, real or imagined, felt by the person with such a sign as Capricorn rising. With this, there is a sense of inadequacy which tends with age, experience, and introspection to dissipate.

The ruling planet of Jung's rising sign is in the sign of Aquarius, in the first house of his natal chart. This position further reinforces his feelings of limitations and inadequacy, and suggests that his father, represented by his Saturn, in the unique sign of Aquarius, would be a major influence in Jung's view of his world.

THE VALKYRIES

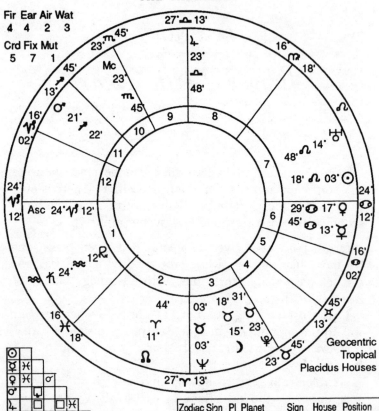

Fir Ear Air Wat
4   4   2   3

Crd Fix Mut
5   7   1

27° ♎ 13'

♃ 23° ♎ 48'

16' ♏ 18'

Mc 23° ♏ 45'

23° ♏ 45'

45'

13°

16' ♂ 21° 22'
02' ♐

24° ♑ 12'

Asc 24° ♑ 12'

24° ♒ 12' ℞

16' ♓ 18'

27° ♈ 13'

♈ 11°

♌ 48' ♅ 14°

18' ♌ 03' ⊙

29' ♋ 17' ♀
45' ♋ 13' ☿

24' 12'

16' 02'

45' 13'

23' ♉

15' 23' ♇

03' ♉ ☽

18' 31' ♉

44' 03'

♉

♏

Geocentric
Tropical
Placidus Houses

Ω

Ψ

Zodiac Sign	Pl	Planet	Sign	House	Position
♈ Aries	☽	Moon	Taurus	3rd	15° ♉ 18'
♉ Taurus	⊙	Sun	Leo	7th	03° ♌ 18'
♊ Gemini	☿	Mercury	Cancer	6th	13° ♋ 45'
♋ Cancer	♀	Venus	Cancer	6th	17° ♋ 29'
♌ Leo	♂	Mars	Sagittarius	11th	21° ♐ 22'
♍ Virgo	♃	Jupiter	Libra	8th	23° ♎ 48'
♎ Libra	♄	Saturn	Aquarius	1st	24° ♒ 12' ℞
♏ Scorpio	♅	Uranus	Leo	7th	14° ♌ 48'
♐ Sagittarius	♆	Neptune	Taurus	3rd	03° ♉ 03'
♑ Capricorn	♇	Pluto	Taurus	3rd	23° ♉ 31'
♒ Aquarius	Ω	Node	Aries	2nd	11° ♈ 44'
♓ Pisces	Mc	Midheaven	Scorpio		23° ♏ 45'
	Asc	Ascendant	Capricorn		24° ♑ 12'

Aspect Name		360	Exact	#
☌	Conjunction	–	000°00	2
☍	Opposition	1/2	180°00	4
△	Trine	1/3	120°00	6
□	Square	1/4	090°00	8
⚹	Sextile	1/6	060°00	7
∠	Semi-Square	1/8	045°00	
⚺	Semi-Sextile	1/12	030°00	6
⚻	Quincunx	5/12	150°00	2
⚼	Sesquiquadrate	3/8	135°00	1

CARL GUSTAVE JUNG
July 26, 1875
Kesswil, Switzerland
07:32:00 pm CET
Zone: -01:00   009E19'00"   47N36'00"

112

The Sun, in the sign of Leo, placed in the seventh house, denotes tremendous potential for self-fulfilment and individuation. The creative potential is tremendous but, it requires co-operation and partnership (seventh house symbolic meaning).

'"Long live the king." The energy is dynamic, solar. In honour of the ruler Sun, the energy instinctively desires public acclaim and approval. As a fixed sign, Leo stands high on a pedestal and surveys the surrounding fields. Magnanimity, warm-hearted generosity are given to the people, as long as the pedestal is high and the dominance assured. Yet assumption of a lofty position can lead to the downfall of any shining leader unless he produces what he promises.

'The energy distribution can manifest as an inspiring leader or a show-off. The range is as great as the energy potentials are vast. The self-reflection can be so true and vivid that arguments, suggestion, ramifications never see light. In Leo, the dimensions of theatricality are very strong. Applause is the way to the Leo heart. The square similarity with Taurus (two fixed signs) would clash: the energies have different natures but similar modes of expression. Maybe 'likes' do repel as in a magnet!

'Overwork and overachievement are difficulties for the Leo, depending on the need shown in the rest of the horoscope. The heart and spine are the parts of the body ruled by the Sun in Leo. . . . '[3]

The personality of Jung is seen through the Moon in the sign of Taurus, which is placed in his third house. The Moon symbolises, in its most basic sense, self-preservation. It represents the emotional nature of the individual and in chart analysis stands for the instincts, the unconscious, the mother, and women in general. It is indicative of the anima and is associated with memories, dreams and imagination.

The Moon in the sign of Taurus is exalted and increases the individual's capacity to nurture not only the Self, but others as well.

We have, within the Ascendant, the Sun, and the Moon, the basic ingredients of the potential for Carl

Gustave Jung. A Leo Sun – energetic, creative, and proud. A Taurus Moon – with his self-preservation tied to a practical, earthy, and stubborn emotional nature. Finally, his view of his world as seen through his Capricorn Ascendant – reflecting limitations felt, ambition, desire for success and recognition through achievement.

For those ingredients to mature, we must look to the aspects formed by the planets to those very important indicators, Ascendant, Sun, and Moon. It is within the aspect formations, house placements, and signs, that the dynamic tensions needed for the potential of the individual to be realised and fulfilled are found.

Looking at Jung's natal chart as a whole, it becomes clear that there are two groupings of planets. A first house Saturn in Aquarius trine to a ninth house Jupiter in Libra, with a Mars in Sagittarius in his eleventh house forming a sextile to both Saturn and Jupiter is the first group.

The second group consists of a third house placement of Neptune in Taurus forming a square aspect with the seventh house Leo Sun, a Moon-Pluto conjunction in the sign of Taurus in the third house with the Moon in square aspect to Uranus in the seventh house in the sign of its detriment, Leo.

What enables the energies to flow and fulfil themselves is Saturn square the Moon-Pluto conjunction from the first to the third house and Jupiter square both Sun in Leo (seventh house) and Venus in Cancer in the sixth house.

The essence of the Self requires nourishment to flourish. The early years of an individual are symbolised by the Moon as Mother and by Saturn as Father. Jung's Saturn-Moon square indicate stresses felt through the parental interaction with himself and between themselves. The needs of the child are felt as not being met by either parent. Saturn (father) in the sign of Aquarius suggests a unique or bizarre interaction and the nurturing Taurus Moon (the mother), suggests the potential for smothering with the possibility of creating a greater alienation between father and son.

In time, the Moon enables Jung to nourish himself and

aids in his understanding of his mother and of women in general. It is the feminine in himself (the anima) with which he is in touch. However, Saturn, symbolically the father and Shadow remains to haunt him.

'The Shadow is symbolised by Saturn, the dark angel or Satan, and here we see that which we fear and that which we repress with the greatest emotional intensity, that is those things which we project and dislike the most in others because we cannot bear to accept them as parts of our own nature.'[4]

'As the child needs to be accepted by his parents, those parts of the Self which do not meet acceptance, or which the child believes will not be accepted by his parents, become repressed. This dark, unacceptable side is the Shadow. . . .'[5]

The impetus to fulfil the ambition of Saturn and gain the acceptance Jung needed, is aided by the conjunction of Pluto-Moon in the sign of Taurus in the third house of his natal chart. It is the self-nourishing emotional nature combined with the will-power of Pluto creating the push to succeed. (Moon-Pluto conjunction square Saturn.)

The planet Pluto symbolises the mysteries of life: sex, birth, and death. It is the potential to regenerate and transform that which is no longer useful in the individual's life. Pluto also symbolises will, and placed in the sign of Taurus:

'Pluto . . . revolutionises the Communication System in general and mental attitudes undergo drastic changes.

'The intellect (lower mind) and perceptions are forced into deeper channels of thought and feelings and made to backtrack until the proper vehicle of transition becomes clear.

'The need to cry out – by speaking, writing (or ranting) – becomes overpowering and with Pluto in the Third House one appears to be fated to stand alone.

'Sense impressions are sensitised: memory patterns reach deep into the subconscious vortex and sense of conscious evolution motivates the behaviour.'[6]

Moon conjunct Pluto:

'Natives with this conjunction have intense feelings and are strong willed where their emotions are concerned. They may display psychic and occult tendencies and a leaning toward a subtle emotional domination of the surroundings. They can have a compelling influence over other people. They are open to superphysical realms of manifestation, but in a more positive manner than those with Moon conjunct Neptune. Their interest in spiritualism or matters pertaining to life after death can make them aware of those who are discarnate.

'There is also a tendency to let the past die and to create entirely new bases for emotional experience. Natives are fearless and willing to take risks, and Pluto, ruling the principle of elimination, death, and rebirth, causes them to seek extreme and drastic changes in their lives. They may deal drastically with their families, bringing about sudden changes in the domestic sphere. Sometimes they alienate women by their brusqueness and tendency to be overbearing.

'Whether this conjunction is expressed in creative genius or in destructive emotionality will depend on the aspects made to it and the horoscope as a whole.'[7]

In order to understand the importance of Jung's Moon in Taurus, and to gain further insight into his personality we look to the Moon-Uranus square from the third and seventh houses. Uranus symbolises the potential of the individual to utilise freedom. Moreover, the energy of this planet indicates sudden and unexpected events. It refers to friendships, hopes, and humanity.

'Uranus in the sign of Leo indicates a generation of people who seek freedom in love and romance. Their ideas about courtship and sex may depart from traditional moral standards, and they are likely to believe in free love.

'Uranus in Leo can give strong will-power and creativity in the arts and sciences, as well as the potential for original kinds of leadership. People with this position seek to create a unique type of expression in order to be outstanding in their endeavours. They can develop new concepts in art, music, and the theatre. Rather than conform to the standards of the society they live in, they prefer to create their own standards. However, there is danger of egotism with this position, as Uranus is in its detriment in Leo; hence they should get involved in matters of social or universal – rather than personal – concern.

'These people can be stubborn, and they have difficulty compromising or co-operating with others. If Uranus is afflicted in this sign, they will insist on having their own way, to the extent that they will completely refuse to co-operate.'⁸

Uranus in the seventh house brings the symbolic meanings of that house, such as marriage, partnerships, close personal friendships, contacts with the public and legal contracts into the area of one's life experiences. Unexpected and sudden changes are certain to occur as the tendency for freedom within these restraints are strong.

To see how the essence of Self (Leo Sun) is tested, we look to the developmental tension of Sun-Neptune square. In the sign of Taurus, Neptune as the ruler of Pisces, a water sign, loses its receptive qualities to earthy practicalities and indicates the potential for inspired thought utilised in nurturing. Neptune as the ruling planet of the natural twelfth house symbolises the ideal of compassion towards all living things without reward. Neptune in the house of the rational mind (third house) presents the potential for delusion or inspiration. The self-deception possibility would be very great without a strong Saturn, which Jung has. And it is the combination of practical, self-nurturing will with inspired thought processes which drives the ambition (Saturn) and gives, through Saturn, the fixity of purpose to transform himself.

Another aspect of tension is the Jupiter in Libra in the eighth house square the seventh house Leo Sun. The eighth house is the natural house of the sign Scorpio, ruled by the natural ruler of Scorpio, Pluto. Jupiter symbolises the potential of the individual to attain wisdom, through travel, education, and experience. Jupiter in

Libra indicates the areas of experience involved in the tension of the aspect. It is basically partnerships or co-operation given and received. A Leo Sun (king) is given co-operation and in the face of refusal, his emotional powerhouse explodes (Moon conjunct Pluto and Moon square Uranus). The lesson to be learned is both one of giving co-operation and curtailing the false pride a Leo Sun has the tendency to express. The self discipline of Saturn must be brought to bear if the Ego is to be fulfilled in its quest for evolutionary enfoldment.

The sixth house placement of Venus in the sign of Cancer is also a source of dynamic tension through the square aspect to Jupiter in the eighth house in Libra. There is much feeling and sensitivity with Venus in the sign of Cancer. The natural ruler of Cancer is the Moon and Venus is the ruling planet of Taurus. Astrologically, these planets are potentially in mutual reception, allowing their energies to manifest more positively.

Venus through its natural rulership of Taurus, the ruler of the natural second house, is associated with the following areas of experience: the individual's sense of values, the ability to accumulate wealth, attraction to and by others, the aesthetic sensibilities, and personal comfort.

The sixth house symbolises service to others, personal health and employment. The sign governing the natural sixth house is Virgo ruled by the planet Mercury which is positioned in the sixth house in the sign of Cancer and thereby dignified.

Within the square aspect of Jupiter and Venus the tension which develops is that personal expansion (Jupiter) suffers when the lack of co-operation given is perceived, thereby resulting in personal discomfort (Venus). The natal chart potential is, for this aspect, to utilise the discipline of Saturn and the judiciousness of Jupiter to transcend the negative results.

Mercury conjunct Venus indicates the potential for Mercury's thought processes (accidentally dignified in the sixth house) to be expressed with great understanding and sensitivity in regard to service to others and through his profession. It is Jung's emotional giving that draws women to him; giving, perhaps, that which he felt he wished to receive.

'Your gentle and easy-going personality is an asset in most professions, but you might find it difficult to cope with the abrasive elements of close and direct competition. This possibility should be taken into consideration when choosing a profession. It is better to work alone or with a small group of people so you won't have to worry about troublesome competition.'⁹

The Leo Sun sextile the Taurus Pluto: '. . . shows that you are fully aware of the intensity of your will. Deep within, you understand that you can accomplish almost anything you want without too much resistance from others. You realise that without knowledge, however, you can't fulfil your destiny. . . .
    'Your ability to communicate your thoughts is so great that others are mesmerised by your words. This ease of communication is your greatest asset. You also have a flair for handling other people's resources, and you easily inspire their confidence in your abilities. Because your talents are so precious, you owe it to the world, as well as yourself, to make them available to everyone.'¹⁰

The energies of Pluto in the sign of Taurus in the third house flow positively and boost the Ego through service to others.
    The sextile of Taurus Moon and Mercury-Venus Cancer symbolises the potential for sensitive and nurturing communication within service to others, which facilitates regeneration and transformation of thought processes and perceptions of others.
    How individuals strive to become empowered and fulfil their potential requires energy, as symbolised by the planet Mars.
    Jung's Mars is positioned in the eleventh house of his natal chart, placed in the Jupiter ruled sign of Sagittarius. (Sagittarius is the natural ruler of the ninth house with the planet Jupiter as its ruler.) Mars represents the manner in which a person asserts himself; it is applied energy

relating to all forms of activity, whether it be in competition, work, or sex. The energy of Mars tends to express itself as all out effort when placed in the eleventh house, especially in regard to the eleventh house areas of hopes, wishes, recognition, and humanitarian concerns. In the sign of Sagittarius the fire of the energy does not burn with the impulsiveness of Aries nor with the brightness of Leo, but has a fervour of its own.

The sextile between Saturn and Mars symbolically gives the individual the mental stamina to lay the foundations and prepare for success. The Jupiter-Mars sextile symbolises the potential for the mental stamina to enhance the aspirations through higher education, travel, and philosophy. Each of these sextile aspects reinforce the trine aspect between Saturn and Jupiter.

The Saturn-Jupiter trine symbolises the easy flow of energies between Jupiter (eighth house of the mysteries of life and other peoples resources; the natural house of Scorpio, ruled by Pluto) in Libra, the sign of partnerships and co-operation given and received, and Saturn in the first house, representing the self as opposed to others.

Within the trine, there is ambition (Saturn) furthered by expansion through use of other people's resources (Jupiter in the eighth).

Carl Jung has six planets in the northern hemisphere of his natal chart, one, Saturn in an air sign; three, Neptune, Moon, and Pluto in earth signs; two, Mercury and Venus in water signs. These placements indicate, especially with Capricorn as a rising sign with Saturn in his first house, that he is considered to be an introvert with an emphasis on intuition and feeling.

Venus, ruled by the Moon (natural ruler of the fourth house of early beginnings) is in a trine aspect to the rising sign and indicates a loving, perhaps doting mother, and is in square aspect with Saturn and indicates tension within the father-son relationship. This is most probably due to the tension Jung feels through his square of Saturn-Moon, indicating tensions between his father and mother.

Jung's perceptions of his world finds its core in these tensions. He is able to see the duplicity and contradictions inherent in human beings, and he turns within himself to resolve those tensions.

The strength of his essence with his Sun in Leo shows that his high level of creativity will take place through the tensions of early life which stimulate his introspection and give impetus to his naturally ambitious nature. He 'will' with Moon-Pluto conjunction, make sense of his life through the high degree of intuition afforded him (Neptune-Moon-Pluto) in the third house of rational thought, combined with his solar creativity so pronounced in the sign of Leo.

The intellectual energy needed for Jung's evolutionary progress is given him through his Mars in the sign of Sagittarius, the higher mind of thought, education and travel. This planet in sextile aspect to both Saturn and Jupiter helps Saturn's ambition through the easy flow of energies between the persistent and unique Saturn in Aquarius and Mars' intellectual energy. Mars, in turn, aids Jung's personal expansion, with the sextile aspect to Jupiter. The trine aspect of Saturn to Jupiter encloses the sextile, creating a dynamic potential for successful striving.

For the release of the energies, we have on the one hand the necessary developmental tensions brought about by Moon and Saturn 'pushing the buttons' of Jung's ambition which stimulate both the Saturn-Jupiter trine and Mars sextile Saturn and Jupiter. On the other hand we have Jupiter square the Leo Sun. The need for recognition and approval is found through determined and creative intellectual accomplishment.

Jung worked his way through the above complexities, starting with the desire to understand himself and then others, and ultimately came to understand himself.

Notes

1. J.L. Brau, *Dictionnaire de L'Astrologie* (English translation by Helen Weaver and Allan Edmands).
2. Ibid.
3. N. Tyl, *The Principles and Practice of Astrology*, Vol. 1.

4. G. Szanto, *Astrotherapy: Astrology and the Realisation of the Self.*
5. Ibid.
6. L. Lowell, *Pluto.*
7. F. Sakoian and L.S. Acker, *The Astrologer's Handbook.*
8. Ibid.
9. R. Pelletier, *Planets in Aspect: Understanding your Inner Dynamics.*
10. Ibid.

Carl Gustav Jung's birth information was obtained from J.L. Brau's *Dictionnaire de L'Astrologie*, which gives a different birth time to Marc Edmund Jones, who gives it as 7.20 p.m. in his *Guide to Horoscope Interpretation*.

The horoscope calculations were made using the computer programme, Blue Star, from Matrix Software, Inc., 315 Marion Avenue, Big Rapids, Michigan. The author wishes to thank Philip Culjak for his comments and interpretations of the chart.

Bibliography

This is a list of all the books given as references. Sources of periodical articles are given in the text.

The Collected Works of C.G. Jung are published by Routledge, Chapman and Hall in the UK and by Princeton University Press in the USA.

G. Adler (ed.), *C.G. Jung: Letters* Vol. 1: 1906–50, Vol. 2: 1951–61. Published by Routledge, Chapman and Hall in the UK and Princeton University Press in the USA, 1973 and 1976.

Berger, M. and Segaller, S., *Wisdom of the Dream*, Shambhala, 1989.
Brau, J.L., *Dictionnaire de l'Astrologie*, Librairie Larousse, 1977.
Brome, V., *Jung: Man and Myth*, Macmillan, 1978.
Campbell, J., *Flight of the Wild Gander*.
Claremont de Castillejo, I., *Knowing Woman*, Harper & Row, 1973.
Down, L., *Freud and Jung: Years of Friendship, Years of Loss*, Scribners, 1988.
Ellmann, R. (ed.) *Letters of James Joyce*, Viking, 1975.
Fielding, C. and Collins, C., *The Story of Dion Fortune*, Star and Cross Publications, 1985.
Fierz-David, L., *Woman's Dionysian Initiation*, Spring Publications, 1988.
The Dream of Poliphilo, Spring Publications, 1986.
Fortune, D., *Psychic Self-Defense*, Aquarian Press.
The Sea Priestess, Aquarian Press, 1957.
Hall, N., *Those Women*, Spring Publications, 1988.
Hannah, B., *Jung: His Life and Work*, G.P. Putnam's and Sons, 1976.
Harding, M.E., *Woman's Mysteries*, Harper & Row, 1976.
Head, R., Rothenberg, R. and Wesley, D. (ed.) *A Well of Living Water*, a festschrift book, privately printed for Hilde Kirsch's 75th birthday, C.G. Jung Institute, 1977.
Huelsenbeck, R., *Memoirs of a Dada Drummer*, Viking, 1974.
Jacobi, J., *The Psychology of C.G. Jung*, Yale University Press, 1973.
Psychological Reflections, Princeton University Press, 1970.
The Way of Individuation, New American Library, 1983.
Jaffe, A., *The Life and Work of C.G. Jung*, Princeton University Press, 1979.

Jung, C.G., *Memories, Dreams, Reflections*, Routledge, Chapman and Hall, 1963.
Jung, E., *Animus and Anima*, Spring Publications, 1969.
The Grail Legend (with Marie-Louise von Franz), Sigo, 1986.
Lowell, L., *Pluto*, Llewellyn Publications, 1973.
Luthi, M., *Once Upon a Time: On the Nature of Fairy-Tales*, Indiana University Press, 1976.
McGuire, W., *The Freud/Jung Letters*, Routledge, Chapman and Hall, 1974.
McGuire, W. and Hull, R.F.C., *C.G. Jung Speaking: Interviews and Encounters*, Princeton University Press, 1977, and Thames and Hudson, 1978.
Ostrowski-Sachs, M., *Conversations with C.G. Jung*, Juris Druck Verlag, Zurich.
Pelletier, R., *Planets in Aspect: Understanding your Inner Dynamics*, Para Research Inc., Gloucester, Massachusetts.
Progoff, I., *Spiritual Disciplines: Papers from the Eranos Yearbooks*.
Richardson, A., *Priestess*, Aquarian Press, 1987.
Sakoian, F. and Acker, L.S., *The Astrologer's Handbook*, Harper and Row, 1970.
Samuels, A., *Jung and the Post-Jungians*, Routledge, Chapman and Hall, 1985.
Schocken, M. and Serrano, M., *Jung and Herman Hesse: A Record of Two Friendships*.
Szanto, G., *Astrotherapy: Astrology and the Realisation of the Self*, Arkana, Routledge, Chapman and Hall.
Tyl, N., *The Principles and Practice of Astrology*, Vol. 1, Llewellyn Publications, 1974.
van der Post, Sir L., *Jung and the Story of our Time*, Atheneum/Pantheon.
Wilson, C., *Lord of the Underworld: Jung and the Twentieth Century*, Aquarian Press, 1984.

Glossary

Archetype a primordial image within each human psyche such as, for example, the Great Mother, the Wise Old Man, the Trickster.

Anima the contrasexual element within the male psyche most easily seen in projection upon women.

Animus the contrasexual element within the female psyche most easily seen in projection upon men.

Collective Unconscious in Jungian psychology this is the part of the unconscious mind made up of instincts and archetypes which are universal.

Extraversion an attitude type in which concentration of interest is on the external object such as people.

Individuation the psychological growth process whereby the impulse towards wholeness is paramount.

Introversion an attitude type in which the concentration of interest is on the inner reality.

Persona the mask or role we assume in accordance with the values and expectations of the society in which we live.

Psychological types Jung's term for the inborn preference of function in life. These preferences are determined through psychological testing with either the Myers-Briggs test or the more recent Wheelwright test. Jung believed that these functions develop and get stronger through use and the inferior, or more unconscious functions may be developed consciously through the individuation process.

Self the central archetype of the personality most often seen in dreams or fantasy material as a sacred child or in the form of a mandala.

Shadow the archetype for those personal characteristics which are kept hidden by us because they are viewed as socially or personally unacceptable or objectionable. Most often seen in projection upon others.

Synchronicity meaningful coincidence within events which have no cause/effect relationship.

Index